AQUARIUM
PLANTS

Comprehensive coverage, from growing them to
perfection to choosing the best varieties.

Peter Hiscock

INTERPET
PUBLISHING

CONTENTS

© 2005 Interpet Publishing,
Vincent Lane, Dorking, Surrey,
RH4 3YX, England.
All rights reserved.

Reprinted 2011

ISBN: 978-1-84286-104-2

Credits
Created and compiled: Ideas
into Print, Claydon, Suffolk
IP6 0AB, England.
Design and Prepress: Phil Kay
Design, Elmdon, Saffron Walden,
Essex CB11 4LT, England.
Photography: Geoff Rogers
© Interpet Publishing
(Also see Credits page 208.)
Production management:
Consortium, Poslingford, Suffolk
CO10 8RA, England.

Printed and bound in China.

Part One: Practical section 6-87

Part Two: Plant profiles *88-201*

Author

Peter Hiscock began keeping fish and aquariums as a child, inspired by his parents, both accomplished marine biologists. He was appointed manager of a retail aquatic outlet at just 17 years of age and went on to complete aquatic studies at Sparsholt College in Hampshire, UK. He entered publishing with contributions to the aquatic press. His main interests include fish behaviour and the interaction of fish with their environment, as well as aquascaping and the natural habitats of aquarium species.

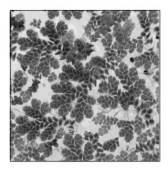

CONTENTS

PART ONE

Understanding aquarium plants

For beginners and newcomers to keeping aquarium plants, there is an increasing amount of information available relating to plant care, and at first glance, it can appear quite daunting. Thankfully, a complete understanding of all the aquatic processes that govern good plant care is not required from the start. It is possible, and probably more useful, to learn as you go along.

The first part of this book focuses on practical matters, beginning with the biological processes that occur within plants and the systems they use to thrive underwater. If you acquire a basic understanding of the biology of plants and their requirements, the rest will follow.

Water quality dictates much of the aquarium environment, and in the water quality and filtration section, the properties of water are examined, along with the processes that occur in the aquarium that alter water quality. Filtration and the types of filter suited to a planted aquarium are also discussed.

The good health of plants depends largely on the environment they are kept in, and preparing this begins well before any plants are introduced. For example, the substrate provides much more than a simple rooting medium for plants, and this topic is examined in detail. Other sections in this part of the book focus on choosing aquatic plants and preparing them for planting, lighting the aquarium, feeding plants and propagating them.

Once planted, you must keep your aquarium display looking its best, so ongoing care and maintenance are discussed next. Finally, we embark on the exciting prospect of aquascaping – how to design a superb aquarium display, using not only plants, but rocks, wood, bark and other decor. And for further inspiration, take a look at the aquascaped display tanks that reflect different environmental conditions and a range of biotopes.

With a little time and patience, a stunning display aquarium is not difficult to achieve; the rewards are well worth the effort involved.

Plant biology

Although there are a few exceptions, plants in general do not consume other organisms to obtain the energy and the basic elements they need to live, grow and reproduce. Instead, they use the processes of photosynthesis to obtain energy, and absorb vital elements directly from the surrounding environment. This simplified way of life has allowed plants to thrive and spread in many habitats, becoming the basis of support for more complex organisms and food chains. Plants are producers rather than consumers; they 'produce' biological material rather than 'consume' it.

Plants developed on land before venturing under water and although aquatic plants are highly adapted to the underwater environment, many of their physical attributes can be traced back to their terrestrial ancestry.

Looking at the biology and structure of aquatic plants, helps us to understand why certain conditions are needed in the aquarium if we want to keep aquatic plants successfully.

Photosynthesis

The unique function that plants possess is the ability to obtain energy from sunlight, carbon dioxide and water, using the process of photosynthesis. Photosynthetic cells within the leaves and stem tissues contain pigments that trap light energy to break down the molecular structure of water (H_2O) into hydrogen and oxygen. The hydrogen binds first to carbon dioxide and then oxygen to form glucose, which is a basic sugar and an important source of energy. Some oxygen is left over from this process and is released back into the water, where it is either used up by bacteria and

Below: Oxygen produced during photosynthesis can be clearly seen on this echinodorus leaf. The oxygen is a waste product and is released back into the water and used by other organisms.

animals for their respiration or released into the atmosphere at the water surface.

The glucose produced from photosynthesis is water soluble and, if stored in large quantities, will absorb water and enlarge the cells that contain it. Obviously, this is undesirable for plants, so the glucose is quickly converted into an insoluble starch compound and transported to various parts of the plant for storage, in most cases to the upper root area. Many plants store starch in tubers, rhizomes and bulbs. The starch can be easily converted back into glucose and transported around the plant when needed for energy or growth.

How photosynthesis works

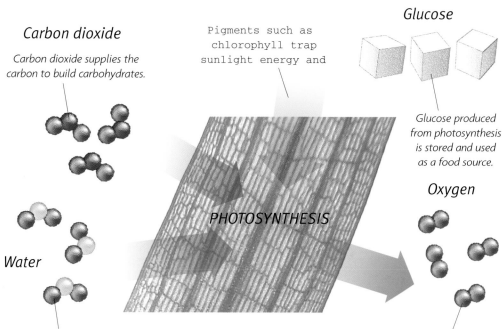

Carbon dioxide

Carbon dioxide supplies the carbon to build carbohydrates.

Pigments such as chlorophyll trap sunlight energy and

Glucose

Glucose produced from photosynthesis is stored and used as a food source.

Oxygen

PHOTOSYNTHESIS

Water

Water is easily absorbed by aquatic plants.

Oxygen is released as a waste product.

Factors affecting photosynthesis

A plant has very little control over the rate of photosynthesis that occurs within its cells. A number of environmental factors are responsible for the productivity of the photosynthetic cells and it is always the factor in least supply that limits the rate of photosynthesis. The aim in the aquarium is to remove the majority of constraints on photosynthesis to obtain the optimum level.

Higher rates of photosynthesis will encourage faster growth, reproduction and improved plant health. Light is the most obvious environmental factor, but temperature, carbon dioxide levels and nutrient availability also affect the rate of photosynthesis. In bright conditions, a plant may receive more light than it needs to produce adequate amounts of glucose. At night, plants stop photosynthesising and only start again in daylight.

Plant biology

Limiting factors on photosynthesis

Right: Assuming that the supply of nutrients and other environmental conditions are correct, three factors affect the rate of photosynthesis: temperature, carbon dioxide (CO_2) and light.

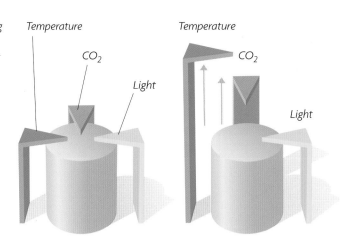

Left: If one factor is in short supply, photosynthesis will be restricted. Increasing the temperature and CO_2 content will not increase photosynthesis if the plants do not receive enough light.

Right: In most aquariums, the CO_2 content of the water is the limiting factor. Even with the correct temperature and good lighting, plants will not grow well if they receive little CO_2.

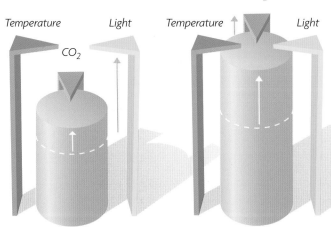

Left: Once CO_2 and lighting levels are sufficiently high, and the temperature is at an optimum level, the rate of photosynthesis will increase rapidly. Mostly, this will produce a healthier aquarium plant.

Respiration and oxygen levels

Respiration helps to break down food sources and release energy into the cells. During the process, oxygen is used up and carbon dioxide is released as a by-product. Respiration is a continual process that does not stop at night. Thus, photosynthesis stores food 'energy', whereas respiration releases energy.

In a heavily planted aquarium, respiration has a significant effect on oxygen levels within the tank. In any 24-hour period, plants release more oxygen through photosynthesis than they use up during respiration. Bacterial organisms also use up oxygen continually through respiration. At night, a heavily planted aquarium can quickly use up oxygen until it is at such a low level that fish begin to suffer from oxygen deficiency. The problem is generally confined to heavily planted aquariums with little aeration or water movement, and can be remedied by increasing oxygenation at night. Plants do not generally appreciate a high oxygen level in the aquarium because it diminishes their ability to obtain nutrients. This means that constant aeration is not beneficial in planted aquariums and should only be employed at night, when oxygen deficiencies may occur. The aim is to balance the needs of the plants and the fishes in a planted aquarium.

How respiration works

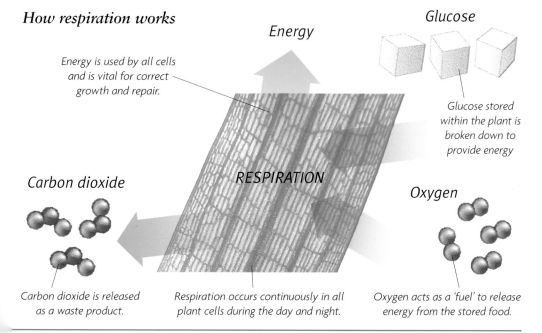

Glucose

Energy

Energy is used by all cells and is vital for correct growth and repair.

Glucose stored within the plant is broken down to provide energy

Carbon dioxide

RESPIRATION

Oxygen

Carbon dioxide is released as a waste product.

Respiration occurs continuously in all plant cells during the day and night.

Oxygen acts as a 'fuel' to release energy from the stored food.

Plant biology

Cell structure

The vital life processes of plants, such as photosynthesis, respiration, nutrient transfer and gas exchange, all take place within individual cells. All cells are made up of the same structural components and it is a variation in these that creates different cells for different purposes.

CO$_2$ is converted into glucose in this nutrient-rich liquid.

Cell nucleus

Respiration occurs in mitochondria.

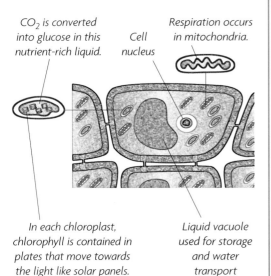

In each chloroplast, chlorophyll is contained in plates that move towards the light like solar panels.

Liquid vacuole used for storage and water transport

Plant anatomy

Although some plants lack a central stem, and plants such as mosses and ferns do not produce flowers, the anatomy of most plants can be split into four basic zones; the roots, stem, leaves, and flowers. All these parts play a vital role in the plant's basic functions, including growth, reproduction, nutrient-collection and storage.

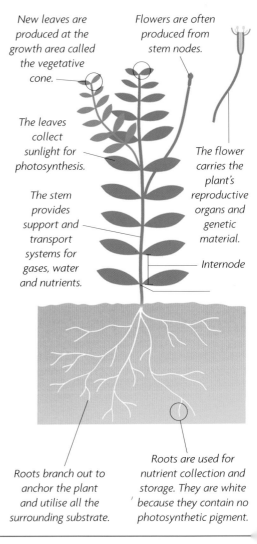

New leaves are produced at the growth area called the vegetative cone.

Flowers are often produced from stem nodes.

The leaves collect sunlight for photosynthesis.

The flower carries the plant's reproductive organs and genetic material.

The stem provides support and transport systems for gases, water and nutrients.

Internode

Roots branch out to anchor the plant and utilise all the surrounding substrate.

Roots are used for nutrient collection and storage. They are white because they contain no photosynthetic pigment.

Types of root

The roots of most aquatic plants are a combination of a number of central roots, up to 1.5mm (0.06in) in diameter, with many smaller roots trailing off. Terrestrial plant roots have fine hairs for trapping moisture, but these are not present in aquatic plants, although they may develop on some bog plants when grown out of water.

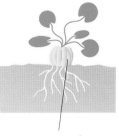

In some roots, the upper part contains nutrients in storage organs.

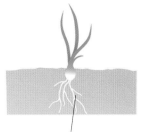

Many plants grow from bulbs or tubers, which contain large reserves of nutrients.

Large plants produce longer and thicker roots for better anchorage and nutrient collection.

Floating plants produce many branched, fine roots that help to assimilate nutrients.

Some aquatic plants produce roots from a rhizome that attaches to rocks and wood.

Plant biology

The function of stems

A stem is present in most aquatic plants and performs two basic functions: support and transport. The stem's function is aided by supporting gas- or air-filled cells that provide buoyancy and help to keep the plant upright. Since the surrounding water provides much of a plant's support, aquatic stems are often much thinner and more flexible than terrestrial stems. Flexible stems allow the plant to move with the water, rather than try to hold steady against it, risking damage.

Leaves

The leaves of a plant are essentially tools for collecting sunlight to use in the process of photosynthesis. Gas exchange and some collection of nutrients is also carried out by the leaves. The leaves of terrestrial plants have a thick, waxy outer layer called the cuticle, which protects the plant from drying out. In aquatic plants this layer is much thinner and liquid is able to pass through much

more easily, which helps the plant to take up nutrients. Aquatic plants that produce aerial leaves often show two different leaf shapes below and above the water. This is due to the different environments and a change in the cuticle layer.

Above: Alternanthera reineckii *needs strong light to maintain its red-brown leaf colour.*

Above: This Saururus cernuus *plant is sending up leaves above the water surface, where they can absorb carbon dioxide directly from the air. The submerged leaves are larger and thinner than the aerial ones.*

These plantlets are produced in small groups on a thick stem runner and will become quite large before they separate and root as genetically identical versions of the parent plant.

Right: *Flowers raised above the main plant are accessible to pollinating insects.*

Below: *The arrangement of leaves in this cryptocoryne enables them to receive maximum light.*

Flowers

Although not all aquatic plants are likely to produce flowers in the aquarium, the majority are flowering plants and will produce seeds and reproduce by flowering in nature. The flowers are usually produced above water, where they can be pollinated by insects, just as terrestrial ones are.

Some aquatic plants produce flowers beneath the water surface. In these instances, the seeds are capable of floating downstream and a few species do not produce flowers at all, preferring to reproduce by purely asexual means.

Water quality and filtration

Pure water is made up from two hydrogen molecules and one oxygen molecule (H_2O). However, the water in which you house living aquatic organisms such as fish and plants is much more than a simple combination of molecules. Water can be described as hard or soft, alkaline or acid, and acts as a carrier for a wealth of minerals, nutrients, toxins, bacteria (both beneficial and harmful) and pollutants. Providing good water quality means ensuring that all these factors are at the correct level, so that the water in the aquarium is not only safe for fish and plants, but actively encourages their health and growth.

Filtration

In all aquariums, you can employ four types of filtration in one way or another: mechanical, biological, chemical and ultraviolet light sterilisation. The function of filtration in the aquarium is to remove or neutralise substances that may be harmful, and to remove visible debris from the water. In nature, a combination of naturally occurring bacteria, organisms and vegetation provide the waste disposal means to keep water quality stable and pollutants at a minimal level. In the aquarium, the ratio of plants and fish to the volume of water is far higher than in nature. This means that there is more waste to be removed than the natural processes can cope with. Artificial filtration is therefore essential if you are to maintain a healthy aquarium.

Mechanical filtration is the physical removal of visible debris from the water and performs a purely aesthetic function. Generally, mechanical filtration is achieved by passing water through a sponge, or series of sponges, to trap debris. These can then be removed and cleaned. In the planted aquarium, mechanical filtration is important because it removes suspended debris that may otherwise collect in the foliage of fine-leaved species. This prevents light from penetrating the chlorophyll cells, reducing their ability to photosynthesise. A build-up of organic debris in the aquarium may also encourage the growth of algae and increase the number of disease-causing bacteria in the aquarium.

Below: *The clear water in this vegetated river gives the impression of a healthy environment, but the elements that create unhealthy water are also invisible.*

How reverse osmosis works

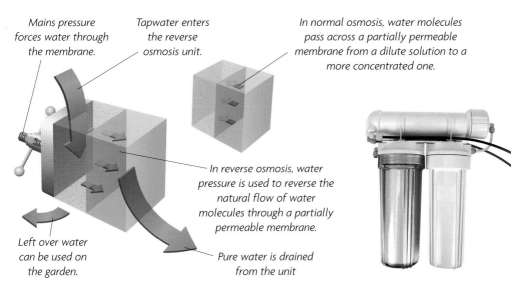

Mains pressure forces water through the membrane.

Tapwater enters the reverse osmosis unit.

In normal osmosis, water molecules pass across a partially permeable membrane from a dilute solution to a more concentrated one.

In reverse osmosis, water pressure is used to reverse the natural flow of water molecules through a partially permeable membrane.

Left over water can be used on the garden.

Pure water is drained from the unit

Reverse osmosis (R.O.) water is also produced by a mechanical filtration unit, although in this case the sponge is replaced by an incredibly fine membrane. This removes almost all the contaminants (meaning everything other than water molecules – H_2O), leaving almost pure water. However, R.O. water is not suitable on its own for fish or plants because it is deficient in some of the important elements of water that provide a stable and useful environment. R.O. water must be mixed either with tapwater or a chemical 'buffer' that introduces trace elements and carbonates to stabilise pH. Water changes are also a form of mechanical filtration as they constitute a physical method of removing substances.

Above: A commercial R.O. unit produces water with a pH of 6.5-7 and no hardness. Add buffers, trace elements and nutrients to sustain plant and fish life.

Biological filtration is the most important filtration process, and involves the breakdown and removal of organic pollutants, such as ammonia and nitrites, by bacteria. A biological filter medium is one with a high surface area on which bacteria can settle and remove pollutants by a process of oxidation. For larger filters and external filters, biological media such as sintered glass or ceramic nodules have a much increased surface area that provides more efficient and balanced biological aquarium filtration.

Water quality and filtration

The nitrogen cycle

In anaerobic (no oxygen) conditions in the substrate, and sometimes in the filter, anaerobic bacteria break up nitrates to obtain oxygen, thus releasing nitrogen gas.

Plants convert light, carbon dioxide and nutrients into biological matter.

Plant material and proprietary foods are consumed by fish.

Fish waste is excreted directly and indirectly as ammonia (NH_3), which is highly toxic.

Nitrosomonas bacteria in the filter and aquarium substrate use oxygen to break down ammonia into nitrites (NO_2).

The majority of nitrates are removed by water changes, although some are converted by substrate bacteria.

Nitrates are only toxic at high levels and are partially taken up by plants as a source of nutrients.

Nitrobacter bacteria in the filter and substrate break down nitrites into nitrates (NO_3).

Nitrites are slightly less toxic than ammonia, but still poisonous, even at very low concentrations.

Chemical filtration removes chemical substances from the water using a medium that binds chemical compounds to itself. This binding is called adsorption and a chemical filtration medium is described as an adsorptive medium. Most chemical media are indiscriminate and will adsorb a wide range of compounds, both good and bad. They remove not only toxins, such as heavy metals, nitrites and nitrates, but also useful compounds, such as nutrients and many aquatic treatments. For this reason, chemical filtration is best employed as a temporary form of filtration. It can be very useful in the removal of disease or algal treatments, once these have done their job, to remove heavy metals such as copper, etc., and to filter rainwater or tapwater before they are added to the aquarium.

Types of filtration unit

Several types of filter are available for aquariums, although most work on the same basic principle. In most cases, water is drawn by a pump through a canister containing filtration media. Most filters are based on either internal or external designs. An internal filter is a compact unit that usually contains a sponge medium used for both mechanical and biological filtration. An external filter also uses sponge media, but because it is placed outside the aquarium it can be much larger without taking up space in the aquarium. The extra space available in the canister of an external filter allows you to use a wide range of media, which makes an external filter much more flexible and adaptable.

Because the bacteria that perform biological filtration require high amounts of oxygen, most filters have a high flow rate, allowing water to pass through the filter before the oxygen is used up. In some cases, this can cause problems for aquarium plants, because high oxygen levels make it difficult for them to assimilate nutrients. In a planted aquarium, it is sometimes best to use filters with lower flow rates, or undersized external filters to reduce the surface movement and keep oxygen levels low. Lowering the outlet of a filter will also help to reduce surface movement in the aquarium.

An internal power filter

This pump unit powers the filter. Clean the impeller periodically.

Filtered water returns to the tank here.

Compartment for activated carbon to remove discoloration and pollutants when needed.

Sponge traps particles and harbours beneficial bacteria. Some internal power filters contain additional biological and chemical media in separate compartments.

Water quality and filtration

Filters with aerobic and anaerobic bacteria

To encourage both aerobic and anaerobic bacteria in filters, allow part of the filter to clog, but keep the rest relatively clear. To do this, have a 'clean' sponge and a 'dirty' sponge in the filter. First, water passes through the clean sponge, where aerobic bacteria reduce ammonia and nitrites and produce nitrates. Next it passes through the dirty sponge, where the nitrate is converted to nitrogen gas.

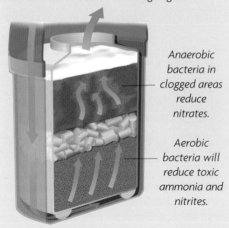

Anaerobic bacteria in clogged areas reduce nitrates.

Aerobic bacteria will reduce toxic ammonia and nitrites.

Acidity / alkalinity (pH)

The pH value is a measure of how alkaline or acidic the water is. The pH level is closely linked to levels of carbon dioxide in the aquarium, because carbon dioxide produces carbonic acid, which is acidic and lowers pH. The pH in most aquariums will drop over time due to the acids produced by waste organic

matter, respiration and filtration processes. Regular removal of waste matter and regular water changes will reduce this effect. Changes in pH are damaging to fish and plants only if they happen suddenly. Because carbon dioxide and organic-rich substrates are used in planted aquariums, the water is more often slightly acidic than alkaline, although fluctuations occur within a 24-hour period due to the photosynthetic and respirational effects on carbon dioxide and oxygen concentrations in the water. Most plants are happy in water with a pH value between 6.0 and 7.5.

How pH is measured

Water (H_2O) is made up of positively charged hydrogen ions (H^+) and negatively charged hydroxyl ions (OH^-). The pH level is a measure of the ratio of these two ions in a body of water. Acidic water has more hydrogen ions; alkaline water more hydroxyl ions. Neutral water has an equal number of both.

WATER MOLECULE

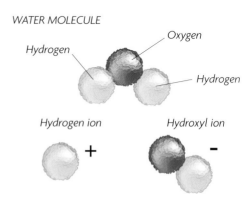

Oxygen

Hydrogen

Hydrogen

Hydrogen ion   Hydroxyl ion

\+   \-

The pH scale

pH is measured on a scale of 1-14, with 7 being neutral. Anything below 7 is acidic and above 7 is alkaline.

The pH scale is logarithmic, meaning that each unit change in pH, say from 7 to 8, is a ten times change. A change of two units from 7 to 9 is a hundred times change, and from 7 to 10 reflects a thousand times change. This is why a sudden change in pH is very stressful and harmful to fish.

pH 9: 100 times more alkaline than pH 7.

pH 8: 10 times more alkaline than pH 7.

pH 7: neutral.

Using liquid test kits

Below: Liquid test kits involve adding a specified number of drops of one or more reagents to a water sample. Hold the bottle vertically so that the drop sizes are equal and correctly measured. Compare the final colour change to a printed chart.

 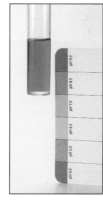

Left: This broad range pH test shows a value of 8.5, reflecting alkaline water conditions. More specific high-range and low-range pH tests are available.

Plants as filters

Aquatic plants also form part of the filtration process in well-planted aquariums. The uptake of metals and nitrogen compounds by plants and the release of oxygen has a significant effect on the overall water quality of the aquarium. In the aquarium, plants are especially useful in removing metals such as copper which may be 'left over' from aquatic treatments. If the function of plants and anaerobic bacteria are included in the nitrogen cycle, filtration in a planted aquarium becomes more complex and efficient.

Water quality and filtration

Water hardness

Water is often described as hard or soft, and these terms relate to the amount of dissolved salts and minerals present in the water. A high concentration of salts and minerals results in hard water, while a low concentration produces soft water. Usually, it is the calcium and magnesium salts that determine overall water hardness. In natural water supplies, hard water usually contains more nutrients than soft water, which is an advantage to aquatic plants. However, hard water generally contains less carbon dioxide and other nutrients in an available form, so plants that are not accustomed to hard water conditions may not do very well in them. A preference for water hardness varies according to species, and in the aquarium it is quite common for aquarists to mix hard and soft water species together. Providing you avoid extremes of water hardness, the majority of plants will do well in medium-soft water with additional carbon dioxide.

Water hardness is often linked with pH, and many of the elements that cause high water hardness also cause a high pH level. However, the two are only loosely connected and it is often possible to achieve high pH levels with soft water.

How hardness affects pH values

Minerals in hard water act as 'buffers' that combine with acids and neutralise them, thus maintaining the hard and alkaline (high pH) nature of the water. Some types of hard water minerals do not have the same effect, as these graphics show.

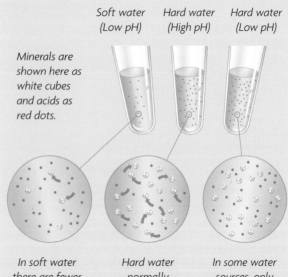

Soft water (Low pH)   Hard water (High pH)   Hard water (Low pH)

Minerals are shown here as white cubes and acids as red dots.

In soft water there are fewer mineral compounds to absorb acids. Soft water is therefore normally acidic and may fluctuate.

Hard water normally contains a number of minerals that bind with acids, maintaining a high pH without fluctuations.

In some water sources, only specific minerals may be present that do not bind with acids. This produces hard water with a low pH.

Sourcing water

Creating the right water conditions can be tricky or easy, depending on the source of the aquarium water. In most cases, this will be tapwater, which varies a great deal according to geographic location. It is vital to test tapwater to find out what qualities it may possess. It is particularly important to test tapwater for both pH and hardness. Although the two are often related, some water companies add substances to the water that may alter one or the other but not both. Tapwater also contains heavy metals, chlorine and, in many cases, chloramine, which releases chlorine over time. Remove these substances before you use the water by adding a simple water conditioner. Then leave the water to warm up a little before using it for water changes, as this will help to minimise temperature shocks to both fish and plants.

To reduce metals and pollutants, and to soften water, tapwater can be mixed with rainwater or reverse osmosis (R.O.) water. Rainwater collected in water butts should always be prefiltered through a chemical medium such as carbon to remove any dangerous substances.

Above: *Tapwater is processed specifically for human consumption. The chemicals added to it by the water company make it safe for us to drink but dangerous to use in the aquarium.*

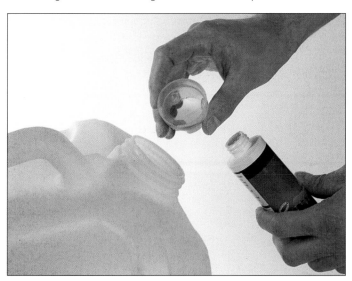

Right: *Before using it in an aquarium, treat tapwater with a dechlorinator that will remove the chlorine and chloramine added by the water company.*

The ideal substrate

In the wild, substrates vary depending on the environmental and geological conditions of the river system and the local area. Aquatic plants are often found in sandy, muddy or gravel beds. In virtually all natural areas, the substrate is usually warmer than the surrounding environment. This happens because the sun's heat is absorbed and retained by the substrate. The difference may be very slight but it is enough to create convection currents between the substrate and the water. These currents slowly and continually move water down through the substrate

(where it warms up slightly) and back up into the main water body, where it cools. As it passes through the substrate it takes nutrients with it, giving the roots access to a continual supply.

The dense muddy substrate found in many places provides an ideal anchoring medium. In natural conditions, the roots may grow far wider and deeper than they could in the aquarium. When keeping some larger plants, take into account that their roots will quickly spread and literally 'take over' the aquarium substrate if allowed to do so.

Nutrient flow in nature

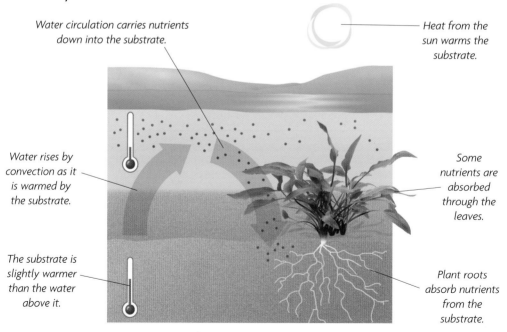

Water circulation carries nutrients down into the substrate.

Heat from the sun warms the substrate.

Water rises by convection as it is warmed by the substrate.

Some nutrients are absorbed through the leaves.

The substrate is slightly warmer than the water above it.

Plant roots absorb nutrients from the substrate.

Below: *In this calm and slow-flowing waterway, sediment is deposited and builds up on top of a rocky bed. Towards the edges, the sediment is deep and provides an ideal substrate for plants to root.*

Substrate heating

As we have seen, the substrate is slightly warmer than the main body of water in natural rivers and lakes. Similar currents can be created in the aquarium using a substrate heating cable. Placed at the base of the substrate, it produces a very gentle heat that raises the temperature of the surrounding substrate. This heat rises through the water in the substrate to the surface and cooler water is drawn down through the substrate so the circulation begins again. The substrate around the heating cable should be fairly dense so that the heat is distributed quickly and the cable is supported and held firmly in place. A very fine substrate such as sand is ideal for this purpose.

A heating cable does not need a thermostat and can be left on continuously. The heat output and power consumption are very low, so the overall aquarium temperature should not be significantly affected. Substrate heating is not a vital part of a good planting substrate, but where thin layers of nutrient-rich substrates are used, the currents produced by a heating cable will significantly improve the distribution of the nutrients.

Below: *The heating cable sits on the base of the tank, where it gently heats the substrate. The coil of heating wire is housed in a plastic sleeve and is designed for use with aquarium plants.*

Left: *Using a jug, pour the washed substrate into the aquarium to a depth of about 7.5cm (3in), taking care not to disturb the heating cable.*

The ideal substrate

Substrates in the aquarium

In an average aquarium, the substrate is likely to be a fairly straightforward affair, usually a simple covering of pea gravel. Plants use the substrate not only as a place to root, but also as a source of nutrients and, in some cases, a medium through which to reproduce. Difficulties encountered when keeping aquatic plants can often be attributed to the lack of a good, useful substrate. Clean, inert gravel creates a fairly biologically inactive substrate. Because the water flows easily through such a medium, it removes nutrients, cools the plant roots and creates an oxygen-rich area, all of which are undesirable and hinder the development of aquatic plant roots.

So which substrates are best? This is not an easy question to answer. Some plants do not need any specialised substrates, while a few species need no

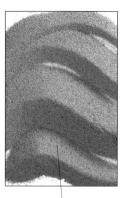   

Silver sand is made up of very fine grains. Its compact nature makes it an ideal medium for heat transfer and a good supportive medium. Ideal as a base layer in the tank when using a heating cable.

Laterite-based substrates act as a long-term source of nutrients. Laterite can be mixed with the main substrate or used as a lower layer, where plant roots are most effective at obtaining nutrients.

Lime-free substrates are made up of inert quartz granules and will not affect water quality in any way. This medium is ideal for supporting roots and should be used as a main substrate.

Pea gravel is the most commonly available aquarium substrate, although it is best used as a top layer in planted aquariums. Smaller grades can be used as a good supportive rooting medium.

substrate at all! However, for the most part, a mixture of substrates will create an environment suitable for all the plants in the aquarium. The points to consider are: the size and shape of the particles, the depth of the substrate layer, and its mineral and organic content.

Size and shape

If the particle size of the substrate is wrong, it may cause problems for aquatic plants. A substrate made up of particles that are too large will allow water to pass through easily, removing nutrients. Furthermore, debris will collect in the gaps between the particles, which may muddy the water. Large-grade substrates also cause problems for the growth of long roots and should only be used as a thin top layer. If the substrate is too fine, it may compact, halting the movement of oxygen and nutrients, and causing damage to the root structure.

A suitable aquarium substrate should have a particle size of about 1-3mm (0.04-0.12in) and be rounded in shape; sharp substrate particles can damage roots. The only exception is sand, which can be used as a thin bottom layer to support heating cables.

Substrate depth

Substrate depth does vary a little, depending on which species you are keeping. Plants that produce long roots, such as *Echinodorus* species and some cryptocorynes, will need a substrate deep enough for the roots to penetrate. If the substrate is too shallow, the roots become tangled and the plant cannot obtain nutrients and the roots will be starved of oxygen. Generally speaking, foreground plants do not produce long roots, so it is possible to slope the substrate upwards towards the back of the aquarium. This also makes the aquarium appear deeper than it is. A good substrate depth is 6-10cm (2.4-4in).

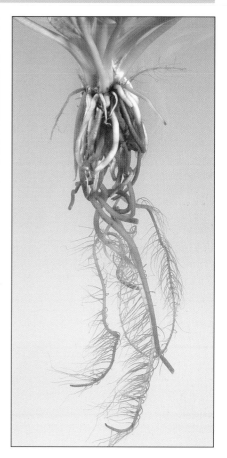

Above: *This echinodorus plant has two distinct root areas: the thicker upper portion is used for nutrient storage, while the thinner lower roots have fine 'secondary' roots used for nutrient collection.*

The ideal substrate

Using soil in the aquarium

Generally speaking, beginners should avoid using soil in the aquarium, as results can vary wildly. However, more experienced aquarists find that soil can be one of the best long-term planting substrates. It contains large amounts of carbon and iron, both readily used by aquatic plants, as well as a number of other nutrients that are slowly released or retained by the soil. If you do decide to use soil, a 2.5-3.75cm (1-1.5in) layer of soil used as a base layer and main substrate, topped with 2.5cm (1in) of fine gravel, will suit most aquariums. The safest strategy is to use only sterilised potting mixture – not garden soil – to prevent contamination.

Left: A mixture of substrates provides a more useful planting medium than a single material. Each substrate has a different function vital to optimum plant health. Here, the bottom sand bed is covered with a nutrient layer and then lime-free gravel.

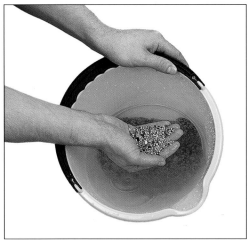

Mineral content

In general, the quantities of minerals required by plants are usually readily available in tapwater. However, if the source water for your aquarium is relatively soft it may be lacking in these minerals, in which case you can use liquid fertilisers (see page 50-51). More importantly, a substrate should not contain harmful minerals, most notably, compounds with a high calcium content. These will increase the alkalinity and pH of the water, making it harder for plants to obtain nutrients and CO_2.

Left: Thoroughly washing gravel substrates is vital to remove dust and debris that will cloud the water. Soil and nutrient-rich substrates do not need to be washed before use,

Organic content

The organic content of a substrate includes organic nutrients, as well as waste matter from the aquarium (mainly from fish). A substrate without any organic matter is simply an 'anchor' for the plants and of little other use. You can add organic matter by using a nutrient-rich substrate, which can either be mixed with the main substrate or arranged as a layer between two substrates.

Above: Soil and peat make excellent planting mediums. They have a very high organic content, so use them with care to avoid overloading the aquarium with organic matter.

Left: Larger grade aquarium substrates allow water to pass easily between the grains, preventing stagnation, although too much water movement in the substrate can be detrimental to good plant growth. The particle size of 3mm (0.12in) used here is a good compromise.

Choosing and planting

Finding a reliable source of healthy plants is vital, especially when you introduce the first plants into the aquarium. Only a small selection of the large variety of aquarium plants may be available from one dealer, so to obtain all the species you require, you may need to locate several suppliers. Choosing different plants and estimating the quantities required takes careful thought and planning. The overall display should be the result of a build-up of plants that gradually become established. They need not all be introduced at the same time; indeed, there are advantages to taking a 'staggered' approach.

Left: You can buy aquarium plants by mail order. They should arrive as here, with the plants in plastic sleeves and slotted into a tray to keep them separate and stable. Sheets of newspaper laid over the top of the outer plastic bag help to insulate them from temperature changes.

Right: The dealer will pack the plants in plastic bags with plenty of air to provide cushioning. The bags are tied to retain moisture, although plants need not be submerged in water.

Identifying healthy specimens is relatively easy and also important, as healthy plants are better able to survive transportation, establish more quickly and live longer once established. Unhealthy plants take far longer to start growing, and if they are in particularly poor condition, may never establish and simply die within a matter of weeks. Once you have selected and bought healthy plants, you must plant them properly and in the correct places to ensure that problems do not develop as they grow and spread.

Even in well-equipped and well-tended planted tanks there are always some plants that do better than others, and a few that simply never 'take' to the aquarium. Bearing this in mind, it is always worth introducing a number of different species to see which ones do better than others. Then you can simply remove and replace the ones that do not thrive with more suitable alternatives.

Choosing a healthy plant

GOOD PLANT

Look for fully formed leaves, with no holes, yellow/brown patches or transparent areas.

Lack of photosynthetic pigment is caused by low nutrient availability.

Here, roots are growing through the pot, along with a few small plantlets and fully formed leaves. This shows vigorous growth and general good health.

BAD PLANT

Bent and broken leaves, along with small holes, are an indication that the leaves on this plant will not last long before they begin to rot.

These roots are not in perfect condition, but given the right environment and providing the roots are intact, even plants in this condition may start to grow new, healthy leaves.

Choosing and planting

Planting vallisneria

Vallisneria creates height at the back of the aquarium. The straplike leaves are quite tough and will not be damaged by the gentle flow from a filter. Before planting, check each plant and remove any brown leaves.

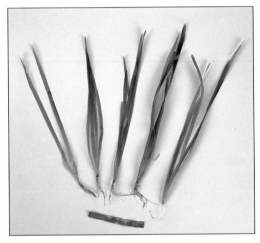

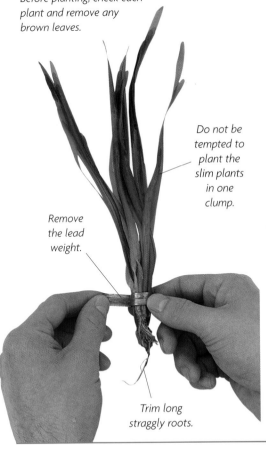

Do not be tempted to plant the slim plants in one clump.

Remove the lead weight.

Trim long straggly roots.

Above: *Removing the lead weight from this vallisneria produces five individual plants, each with healthy roots. Plant them separately, leaving space between them to allow for growth.*

Left: *Gently hold the plant near the base and, using a finger of the same hand, make a hole in the substrate. Slide the plant into the hole, just deep enough to prevent it coming loose.*

Planting ludwigia

1 Carefully unravel the rockwool. There may be as many as three pieces of rockwool, each containing two or three plants. Some aquarists prefer to remove as much rockwool from the plant as they can without causing damage. If this is difficult, expose only the base of the roots, leaving the remaining rockwool intact.

2 Supporting the plant lightly, use your fingers to create a dip in the substrate and hold it open. Try to disturb the substrate as little as possible during planting.

3 Use the remaining substrate to cover the surface of the roots and compact around the base of the stem, just as you would with a terrestrial plant in the soil.

4 Place the same plants close together. Here they are 2.5-5cm (1-2in) apart. Alternatively, leave room so the tips of leaves on separate plants just touch.

Choosing and planting

Planting an echinodorus

1 The base of the plant, normally embedded in a rockwool planting medium, should be gently 'eased' from the pot. Trimming away excess roots first may help.

2 Trimming the long roots reduces any damage caused by planting. Once in the substrate, the plant will respond by quickly producing new and healthier roots.

3 Remove any leaves that show signs of damage. The leaf 'stem' can be gently pulled away from the base. This will not cause any long-term harm to the plant.

4 Putting the plant in place is much like terrestrial planting. Hold the plant gently in one hand and create a dip in the substrate with the fingers of the same hand.

5 Place the roots in the hollowed out area and surround the base of the plant with substrate. Be sure to cover the white area at the base of the plant.

Planting a cabomba

1 Remove the lead weight and separate the cuttings. Take care, as cabomba is a delicate plant that bruises easily and may rot at the base.

2 Using a pair of sharp scissors, cut away the bare stem just below a leaf joint. For shorter pieces, cut further up the stem.

3 Put in each plant individually. Space the plants so that their leaves just touch and light can reach the substrate. Start planting at the rear of the aquarium and work carefully towards the front. Take care not to pull out the plants that are already in place. Avoid placing cabomba in the direct flow from the filter.

Choosing and planting

Attaching Java fern to bogwood

Some aquatic plants, including Java fern, prefer to be planted on objects such as wood and porous rocks, rather than in the substrate. Many of these 'object-rooting' species will also grow, at least partially, out of water and can be raised to the upper reaches of the aquarium and allowed to grow through the surface.

1 *Removing the rockwool from Java fern can be tricky, as the roots are often dense and tangled. However, with a little care, any plant damage can be limited. Try not to keep the plant out of water for too long.*

If there is room, add other plants, such as dwarf anubias and Java moss.

Always choose specimens with healthy leaves, as they grow away more quickly.

2 *To minimise damage and encourage regrowth, trim any excess root with sharp scissors, leaving 1-2cm (0.4-0.8in). Take care not to cut or damage the rhizome (the main root).*

3 *Set the plant on the wood in a natural position. Tie the root firmly but gently to the bogwood with black cotton, which will be hardly noticeable and soon covered by new roots.*

Above: Once it has become established on a piece of bogwood, a Java fern can develop into a focal point in the display. Raised above the substrate, it shines in the lights and provides welcome height.

Lighting for aquarium plants

Plants use light to photosynthesise – a vital process that allows a plant to create its own energy (food) reserves. Without sufficient light, photosynthesis will be impaired and plant health will diminish. Providing a suitable light source, combined with good environmental conditions, will ensure that plants are able to photosynthesise at an optimum rate and remain healthy. In most aquariums, a single fluorescent tube is the norm, but unfortunately, this fails to meet the light requirements of many plants. Correct lighting in general is an area where many aquarium plants suffer. To provide the correct light source for aquarium plants it is important to understand how plants use light in nature and what qualities light possesses.

a significant depth. High-energy light with shorter wavelengths (blue and ultraviolet light) is not as quickly absorbed, so plants are more likely to receive greater quantities of blue light than red.

The photosynthetic pigment chlorophyll, used by the majority of plants for photosynthesis, 'traps' mostly blue and red light, although it is most efficient at trapping red light at around 650-675nm. Blue light is used just as much as red light simply because it is far more available, is stronger in natural sunlight and passes through water more easily. In the aquarium, artificial light should peak, ideally, in the red area of the spectrum, although this can produce an undesirable appearance. Artificial light

Colour is important

Plants use only some of the light they receive, concentrating on specific areas of the spectrum and using only certain wavelengths, usually those that are most readily available. As light passes through water, its intensity decreases but some areas of the spectrum pass through water more easily. Shorter wavelengths of light are more 'energetic' than longer wavelengths and it is the more energetic light that is able to pass through water more quickly. Less energetic light passes through water slowly and is quickly absorbed, so it is not much use to plants submerged at

How plants use light

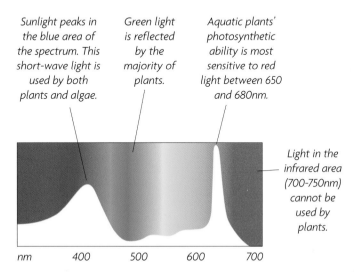

Sunlight peaks in the blue area of the spectrum. This short-wave light is used by both plants and algae.

Green light is reflected by the majority of plants.

Aquatic plants' photosynthetic ability is most sensitive to red light between 650 and 680nm.

Light in the infrared area (700-750nm) cannot be used by plants.

nm   400   500   600   700

Light zones of a river

In a typical river or large stream, there are zones of light and water depth where different plants grow. Cryptocorynes, for example, are ideally suited to the shallow depths of tropical streams. Echinodorus plants, on the other hand, are often found growing up to and above the water surface in the central zones of shallow tropical rivers.

In shallow water, shaded by overhanging vegetation, plants are small and slow growing, needing little rooting depth and less light

Once the water gets a little deeper, plants grow longer roots and thicker stems. They produce large aquatic and aerial leaves, which can use strong light and CO_2 from the surface.

Towards the centre, the water is faster flowing and the light is bright. The plants here have flexible stems that bend with the flow, so aerial leaves are rarely produced.

with a strong blue and red spectrum, is often much more appealing to our eyes and will still provide the plants with suitable light. It is worth remembering that strong blue light will also promote algal growth, so aim for a balance of red and blue light.

Right: In some areas of the Amazon River, the water is crystal clear and the sunlit shallows are brimming with aquatic plants of all kinds.

Lighting for aquarium plants

Light duration

Most tropical regions receive roughly 12 hours of daylight, with ten hours of strong light and ten hours of complete darkness, and this daylength varies little throughout the year. It is important to make sure that plants in the aquarium receive a similar amount of light on a regular basis. Use a timer that automatically switches on the aquarium lights for 10-14 hours a day. In aquariums with, say, a number of fluorescent tubes, you can adopt a 'staggered' approach, with each light being turned on (or off) in a sequence, five to ten minutes apart. This will benefit both the fish and the plants by reducing the shock of a sudden change in light intensity. It is also important that aquarium plants receive periods of complete darkness. During this time, plants stop photosynthesising but continue to respire, so a dark period can be considered a period of 'rest' for the plants' biological functions.

It is possible to combat algae in the aquarium by controlling the intensity and period of lighting and creating a 'siesta' period. This is a period of darkness that interrupts the normal day/night light cycle.

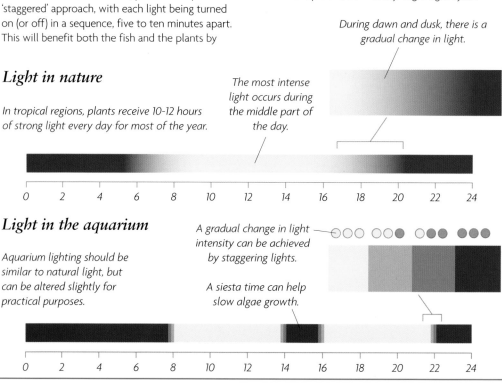

During dawn and dusk, there is a gradual change in light.

Light in nature

In tropical regions, plants receive 10-12 hours of strong light every day for most of the year.

The most intense light occurs during the middle part of the day.

Light in the aquarium

Aquarium lighting should be similar to natural light, but can be altered slightly for practical purposes.

A gradual change in light intensity can be achieved by staggering lights.

A siesta time can help slow algae growth.

How light is lost in the aquarium

In most cases, maximising the amount of light plants receive has a beneficial effect, but there are many ways in which light is lost in the aquarium.

Light from a fluorescent tube is emitted in all directions.

Reflectors help to redirect light into the aquarium.

Some light is refracted and/or reflected from the water surface.

Condensation trays must be kept clean to reduce light absorption.

Particles in the water will 'soak up' a large amount of light.

As light passes through the water, its spectrum is altered and intensity is reduced as it is absorbed and converted into heat energy.

Some light is lost through the aquarium glass.

Plants towards the bottom of the aquarium receive only a small proportion of the emitted light.

Large-leaved and tall plants take up light in the upper areas of the aquarium and reduce the light reaching smaller and/or lower plants

Lighting for aquarium plants

Choosing lighting

When choosing the correct lighting for a particular system, the four main factors to consider are:

1 Efficiency (output in relation to power consumption)
2 Output/Intensity
3 Initial cost
4 Light spectrum

Fluorescent lighting

Fluorescent tubes emit light by electrically charging a gas contained within the tube. The light produced by the gas is mostly in the invisible areas of the spectrum, but the fluorescent coating on the inside of the tube converts this into visible light. By altering the chemical coating on the inside of the tube, the spectrum of light emitted can be changed, so fluorescent tubes can be designed for specific purposes and to emit specific colours. Fluorescent tubes designed for aquarium plant growth often produce a red-yellow or red-violet-blue colour, which although ideal for plants, may look slightly

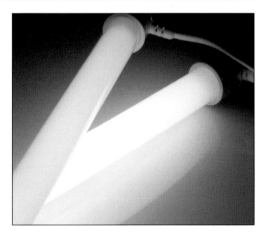

Above: *Fluorescent tubes are available in different colour spectrums for different purposes. Here, a pink 'plant tube' and a white triphosphor side by side.*

Below: *The pink hue created by a 'plant-friendly' fluorescent tube (left) and the more realistic effect from a white, full-spectrum tube (right). Combining these gives the best balance for plants and viewing.*

Below: *The spectral output of a white triphosphor fluorescent tube peaks at 400 and 600nm, ideal for photosynthesis, and at 500nm, which creates a more balanced light appearance for us to view.*

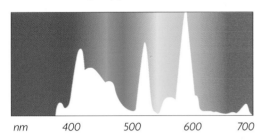

nm   400   500   600   700

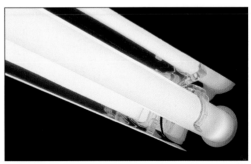

Above: *Fluorescent tubes emit light in all directions. Using a reflector can redirect light into the tank and improve light intensity. These reflectors are made of mirror-finish flexible plastic or polished aluminium.*

garish to our eyes. To remedy this, full spectrum tubes can be added to 'balance' the colour output.

Fluorescent tubes are widely used to light aquariums, mainly because they are very efficient, use little electricity and are relatively cheap when used in small numbers. However, bear in mind that their light output drops considerably within the first year of use, and they should be changed at least once a year. Fluorescent tubes are by far the best lighting solution for smaller or shallow tanks, but for deeper or larger tanks or for plants that require intense lighting, there are other alternatives.

Although light is measured in lumens and lux, fluorescent tubes vary in the intensity and output of light depending on the chemical coating used inside the tube and are rarely labelled in lumens or lux. Fluorescent tubes can be adequately rated for most purposes by the wattage of the light tube rather than its output of light. In aquariums that are 38cm (15in) deep or less, use 1.5-2 watts of light for every 4 litres (about 1 gallon) of aquarium water.

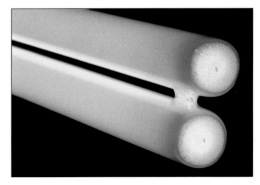

Above: *Biax fluorescent lighting systems incorporate twin tubes close together to produce an intense light for the space they occupy. Another benefit of these lamps is that the tubes can be coated with different phosphor formulations, making it possible to recreate the effect of two separate (and different) tubes in one fitting.*

Lighting for aquarium plants

Metal-halide lamps

Metal-halide, or halogen, lamps provide intense, high-output light via a tungsten filament. They are ideally suited to deeper aquariums, with a water depth of 60cm (24in) or more. Suspended at least 30cm (12in) above the aquarium to allow ample ventilation, a single unit will illuminate approximately $1800cm^2$ ($2ft^2$) of surface area – an aquarium measuring 60cm/24in long and 30cm/12in wide. Halogen lights are usually available in 150-watt or 250-watt versions; a 150-watt light should provide a suitable output for most aquariums. (250-watt versions are better suited to marine invertebrate aquariums, where demand for light from corals is higher.) You may need more than one lamp for aquariums longer than 107cm (42in). Halogen lights are initially the most costly method of lighting, but provide the best output for demanding aquarium plants.

Above: Metal-halide lamps for aquarium use are fitted into housings such as this and suspended above the open tank. They need ventilation space around them because of the heat they generate.

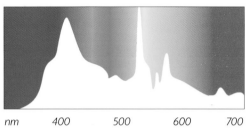

| nm | 400 | 500 | 600 | 700 |

Above: The spectral output of a metal-halide lamp shows useful peaks in the blue and yellow areas. The large (white) volume of the curve reflects the high light intensity these lamps produce.

Mercury vapour lamps

Like halogen lamps, mercury vapour lamps are suspended above the aquarium and provide a high-intensity light that is able to penetrate deeper water than fluorescent tubes. For aquariums with a depth of 45-60cm (18-24in), mercury vapour lamps provide the most cost-effective and practical solution, as they are cheaper than halogen lamps and provide a much higher output than fluorescent tubes. They also produce an aesthetically attractive light.

Common mercury vapour lamps use between 60 and 125 watts, which makes them relatively low-cost to run. If they are within your budget, halogen lamps will provide the best source of light, but mercury vapour lamps are an excellent low-cost alternative.

Above: *In a darkened room, a well-illuminated aquarium provides a stunning, eye-catching feature.*

With a little care, it is possible to achieve the right balance of lighting for the plants, fish and our eyes.

Feeding aquarium plants

Plants require a number of organic and mineral nutrients in order to maintain steady growth and good general health. Most of these nutrients are only required in tiny amounts but without them, vital biological functions cannot be carried out properly. Nutrients can be considered as a plant's 'diet'; without a proper diet, health problems arise and the plant will become 'ill'. The number of nutrients that any given plant requires is extensive and can be provided in a number of ways. Looking at the function of various nutrients, their availability in the aquarium and assessing their importance is a good way of devising a 'shopping list' for suitable sources of fertilisation.

Macro- and micronutrients

Plant nutrients are often described as macro- or micronutrients, depending on the quantities of a particular nutrient required by a plant.

Macronutrients are required in the greatest quantities; these include calcium, carbon, hydrogen, magnesium, nitrogen, oxygen, phosphorus, sulphur and potassium. Many macronutrients are readily available in the aquarium; for example, oxygen and hydrogen are normally always present in more than sufficient quantities, whilst calcium and nitrogen are usually present. Calcium is only found at low levels in very soft water and nitrogen can be absorbed by plants in the form of nitrates and ammonium, which are normally present as a result of biological filtration or from fish/organic waste. Therefore the only macronutrients that the aquarist normally needs to supply are carbon, magnesium, phosphorus, sulphur and potassium.

Micronutrients are only required in very small quantities and are often described as trace elements. Micronutrients include boron, copper, manganese, molybdenum, chlorine, nickel, iron and

Left: A heavily planted display aquarium needs a constant supply of suitable nutrients to keep the plants healthy and growing well.

Signs of nutrient deficiency

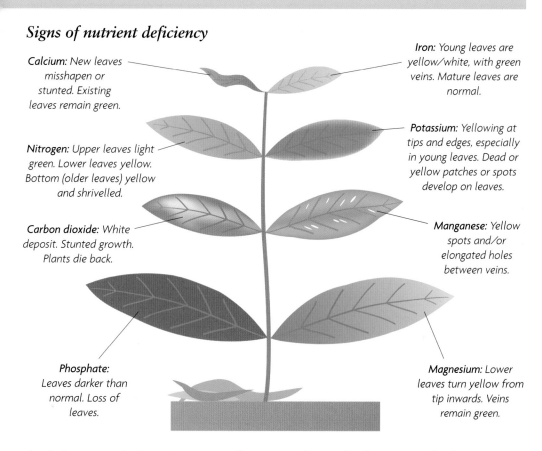

Calcium: New leaves misshapen or stunted. Existing leaves remain green.

Iron: Young leaves are yellow/white, with green veins. Mature leaves are normal.

Nitrogen: Upper leaves light green. Lower leaves yellow. Bottom (older leaves) yellow and shrivelled.

Potassium: Yellowing at tips and edges, especially in young leaves. Dead or yellow patches or spots develop on leaves.

Carbon dioxide: White deposit. Stunted growth. Plants die back.

Manganese: Yellow spots and/or elongated holes between veins.

Phosphate: Leaves darker than normal. Loss of leaves.

Magnesium: Lower leaves turn yellow from tip inwards. Veins remain green.

zinc. Both macro- and micronutrients are equally vital to the overall health of aquatic plants. Whereas macronutrients are usually used for structural components, such as cells, proteins and fats, micronutrients are used for cellular functions and the activation of vital enzymes. Micronutrients can be considered as important for the correct 'management and control' of plant biology. 'Trace elements' can be found in many liquid fertilisers, as well as in most tapwater sources, but are often used up quickly in aquariums both by plants as nutrients and through binding to organic molecules.

Feeding aquarium plants

Sources of nutrients

In the aquarium, nutrients can be supplied to plants from a number of sources. Because plants take up nutrients both through their leaves and the roots, nutrients should be made available in the substrate and the water. Micronutrients, or trace elements, are only needed in small amounts and are often present in most tapwater supplies. However, some may quickly bond with other elements, making larger molecules that are unavailable to plants. They may also need to be supplied in quantity in the substrate or additionally through liquid fertilisers added to the water.

The major difference between liquid and substrate fertilisation is that liquid fertilisers may need to be replaced weekly or every two weeks, whereas substrate fertilisers are normally present for longer periods. The tank substrate acts as a 'storage' facility for some nutrients. The lack of high oxygen levels and water movement in a compact substrate will prevent nutrients from being moved around, oxidated, bonded with carbonates or otherwise made unavailable to plants. In addition, the high amount of organic matter in most substrates allows natural chelates to bond with nutrients, allowing a large quantity of nutrients to be present, while a slow release reduces the amount of 'available' nutrients. Substrate fertilisation can be achieved using proprietary substrate mixes or tablet fertilisers (shown on page 50).

Chelated nutrients

Many nutrients bind with oxygen and other elements, becoming too large to pass through the plant's semi-permeable membrane. These nutrients are of no use to plants.

Large numbers of chelated nutrients are present when an artificial chelate or liquid fertiliser is added. They are small enough to be taken in by plant leaves above the substrate.

Plant roots extend deep into the substrate and release chemicals that aid nutrient assimilation.

Nutrients stripped of oxygen by anaerobic bacteria bind with organic chelates, making them easy for plants to absorb.

Nutrient-rich substrates

Ready-made, nutrient-rich additives are widely available and usually designed as a main substrate, or to be mixed with a small-grade inert substrate. These substrates are high in many of the nutrients required by plants and not commonly available through other sources (tapwater, natural processes, etc.). In an established aquarium, most of these nutrients are released slowly over long periods of time, making nutrient-rich substrates an ideal long-term fertilising solution. Most nutrient-rich substrates will only begin to run out of nutrients after two to three years. However, if you carry out regular small water changes and allow some organic waste to build up in the substrate, it will naturally become a 'sink' for trapping and slowly releasing nutrients indefinitely. Regular small water changes and liquid iron fertilisation should be enough to continually 'recharge' an established substrate that incorporates a suitable nutrient-rich additive.

Using a nutrient-rich substrate

Clay-based substrates, often called laterite, are available that contain a multitude of vital nutrients and trace elements. Most of these are soil-like in appearance and must be 'sandwiched' between two layers of substrate that hold the nutrient-rich medium in place. If allowed to escape, some of the laterite may float and muddy the water. You only need a thin spread of this additive to provide significant benefits for the plants.

1 *Add laterite evenly over the entire surface of the substrate, scattering it from the container in a side-to-side pattern.*

2 *Work methodically from one side of the tank to the other for an even spread.*

3 *Crumble the supplied bacterial culture between your fingers and add a thin layer on top.*

4 *Gently mix the ingredients into the substrate with your fingers and smooth out the top.*

5 *Add a final layer of substrate to create a finished depth of about 10cm (4in) across the aquarium.*

Feeding aquarium plants

Tablet fertilisers

Tablet fertilisers provide a localised supply of nutrients. They are concentrated forms of nutrient-rich substrate additives and particularly high in iron. Some faster-growing plants use vast amounts of iron, and supplying a concentrated source at the roots will help to prevent iron deficiency problems. Deficiencies in other plants, which may not be able to compete for available iron as quickly, will also be reduced or prevented. Do not use tablets as a 'whole-aquarium' solution to universal fertilisation or iron fertilisation, but only to provide an additional source of nutrients for individual plants. Tablets are not required, even locally, when soil-based substrates are used.

Adding a tablet fertiliser

Left: A tablet fertiliser placed close to the roots releases nutrients into the substrate, providing a rapid and long-lasting boost to growth.

1 Tablet fertilisers supply nutrients directly to the roots. 'Greedy' plants that need plenty of iron will benefit from this method of fertilisation.

2 Tablet fertilisers are supplied in blister packs. Pop one tablet out of the pack and place it on the substrate near the roots of the plant.

3 Push the tablet into the substrate under or close to the roots so that they can easily absorb the essential nutrients as the tablet breaks down.

Liquid fertilisers

Several 'off-the-shelf' liquid fertilisers are available for aquatic plants, but they should be used with caution because over-fertilisation can cause problems with algae and metal toxicity. Generally speaking, you get what you pay for when you buy liquid fertilisers; some of the more specialised products are far more valuable and contain the correct quantities of the required nutrients without oversupplying or lacking some elements.

Liquid fertilisers can be particularly useful in supplying chelated iron to the aquarium. Although

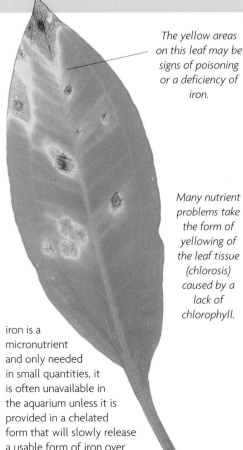

The yellow areas on this leaf may be signs of poisoning or a deficiency of iron.

Many nutrient problems take the form of yellowing of the leaf tissue (chlorosis) caused by a lack of chlorophyll.

Above: *Pour a measured dose of fertiliser into the water. Do not be tempted to add more than directed. Over-fertilisation can be just as harmful as not feeding enough.*

iron is a micronutrient and only needed in small quantities, it is often unavailable in the aquarium unless it is provided in a chelated form that will slowly release a usable form of iron over long periods. Many of the nutrients in liquid fertilisers will become unusable after a short period, usually through binding with other elements or through oxidation. For this reason it is important to dose the aquarium on a regular basis, normally weekly or fortnightly.

Feeding aquarium plants

Carbon dioxide fertilisation

In most planted aquariums, CO_2 fertilisation is vital for plant health and is often the limiting factor in overall growth. Without adequate levels of CO_2, plants cannot photosynthesise effectively and therefore cannot produce the energy needed to perform basic physiological functions. There are several ways of introducing CO_2 into the aquarium. It is created naturally through fish and plant respiration, but mostly by bacteria as they break down organic matter. Many soil-based and established substrates continually release CO_2, which can be used by aquatic plants. However, the quantities produced by these processes are minimal and would not be enough for heavily planted tanks.

This is why additional fertilisation is essential. Furthermore, the air/water exchange in an aquarium continually releases a large quantity of CO_2 into the atmosphere that must be replaced. Various devices designed to introduce CO_2 into the aquarium are available for hobbyists and these include those using tablets that slowly release CO_2, slow-release chemical reactors and pressurised CO_2 cylinders that can be adjusted and set by timers. All these systems introduce CO_2 gas directly into the aquarium water. The aim is to keep the gas in contact with the water long enough for it to be available for plants to absorb.

Left: A plastic fermentation container, water pump, yeast and tubing make up this CO_2 kit.

Introducing CO2 gas

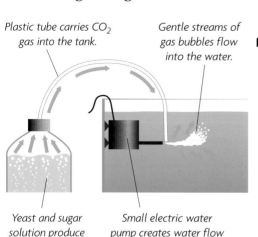

Plastic tube carries CO_2 gas into the tank.

Gentle streams of gas bubbles flow into the water.

Yeast and sugar solution produce CO_2 gas.

Small electric water pump creates water flow to distribute CO_2 gas.

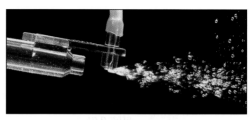

Above: Bubbles of CO_2 gas from the nozzle are circulated by the water pump.

How CO2 cylinder fertilisation works

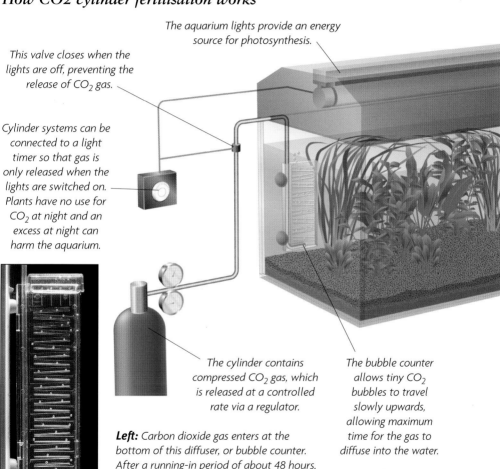

The aquarium lights provide an energy source for photosynthesis.

This valve closes when the lights are off, preventing the release of CO_2 gas.

Cylinder systems can be connected to a light timer so that gas is only released when the lights are switched on. Plants have no use for CO_2 at night and an excess at night can harm the aquarium.

The cylinder contains compressed CO_2 gas, which is released at a controlled rate via a regulator.

The bubble counter allows tiny CO_2 bubbles to travel slowly upwards, allowing maximum time for the gas to diffuse into the water.

Left: Carbon dioxide gas enters at the bottom of this diffuser, or bubble counter. After a running-in period of about 48 hours, the bubbles stabilise and become smaller as they rise and release CO_2 gas into the water.

Propagating aquarium plants

In a healthy aquarium environment, many common aquarium plants will propagate themselves without any intervention from the fishkeeper. Other plants, often those with central stems, can be propagated by a number of artificial methods. Propagation is a good way of increasing the number of plants in the aquarium, as well as replacing old or tattered ones.

Below: The flowers of some aquarium plants are quite stunning in design. Spathiphyllum wallisii *produces blooms that are robust and well able to withstand environmental pressures, both above and below the water.*

Sexual propagation

In the wild, many aquatic plants reproduce sexually, much like terrestrial plants, by producing flowers and seeds, or spores. When a flower is pollinated with the pollen from another plant of the same species, a viable seed is produced with the potential to grow into a new plant. The combination of genetic information from the two parent plants will produce a genetically different plant. Sexual propagation requires two or more plants to produce flowers above the water surface, and although this does occur in the aquarium if the environmental conditions are favourable, it is difficult to control. First you must encourage the plants to produce the strong aerial stems on which the flowers will be borne, so provide a well-ventilated area above the aquarium and below the light unit. Most plants that can produce aerial flowers will eventually do so, although this does depend on the water level, which may have to be lowered for some species. Most stem plants and lilies will produce flowers in the aquarium under the right conditions.

Once the flowers are produced they must be pollinated. In nature, insects transfer pollen, both in aquatic and terrestrial plants, but to carry out the process artificially, transfer pollen from the stamen (male) to the stigmas (female) using a fine artist's brush. In some cases, pollen can be used to fertilise the same plant from which the pollen was taken, thus creating seeds with an identical genetic makeup. If pollination is successful and seeds are produced, plant them up immediately, as often they do not last long before starting to germinate. Many plants can be started off by sprinkling seeds on damp soil, rather than submerged in water, and grown out of water until the seedlings are about 10cm (4in) tall. Others need to have water added gradually, as shown in sequence below.

Right: Barclaya longifolia *(the orchid lily) can only be propagated by seed. At this stage, the seeds are ready to be removed and sown in damp substrate. Most should sprout and produce new plants, which can eventually be moved into an aquarium.*

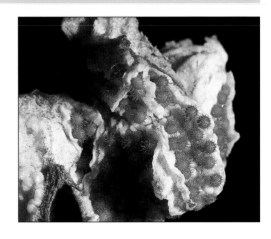

Propagating aquarium plants from seeds

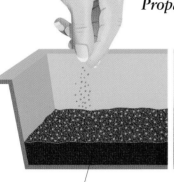

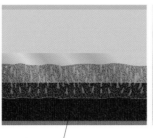

The seeds of most aquatic plants are quite delicate and need not be planted deep in the substrate. Simply sprinkle them onto damp soil.

As the seeds begin to sprout, add a little water so that the leaves are just covered. Some aquatic plants can be grown from seed above water and then transferred directly to the aquarium.

As the new plants grow, raise the water level so that the leaves remain covered. Once the seedlings have at least four or five leaves and are about 10cm (4in) high, they can be moved into the aquarium.

Propagating aquarium plants

Asexual propagation

Most aquatic plants propagate themselves asexually, by which the parent plant produces genetically identical 'daughter' plants. You can encourage the process and ensure the survival of new plants. Aquarium plants reproduce asexually by means of runners, offsets and adventitious plantlets.

Runners Runners are horizontal branches produced at the base of the plant that develop daughter plants (called slips) at the ends. The rootlike runners normally grow just above, or sometimes just below, the surface of the substrate and may continue to extend, producing slips along the runner at intervals of about 6-15cm (2.4-6in). The new slips obtain most of their nutrients from the parent plant and quickly produce roots and new leaves, eventually anchoring in the substrate and becoming completely formed adult plants. The runners between the parent and new adult plants may break down or stay attached and continue to grow new slips. Each new slip produces a new segment so that a chained runner develops, rather than a long, single one.

To remove a daughter plant, cut and shorten the runner and trim the roots on the new plant before replanting it. The new plant should be at least a quarter of the size of the adult plant before it is removed. Detaching daughter plants may prevent the runner from continuing to produce new slips. A good method of selecting new plants is to allow the runner to produce several slips and then remove and replant the healthiest and/or fastest-growing ones.

Propagating from a runner

1 Once the 'mother' plant has produced a number of daughter plants with at least two or three leaves each, simply cut the runner with a pair of sharp scissors.

2 Separate the individual plants, or 'slips', leaving a small length of runner on either side. Handle them carefully, holding them by the leaf and not by the stem.

3 Put each new plant into the substrate, as described on page 33, leaving a gap of at least 5cm (2in) between the plants to allow for future growth.

Many floating plants also produce new plants on runners, although these should be left attached until the runner breaks down naturally. This will happen when the new plant is sufficiently well developed to survive on its own. Common species of aquarium plants that propagate by runners include *Cryptocoryne, Echinodorus, Sagittaria, Vallisneria* and some floating species.

Offsets Offsets are produced in a similar way to runners, but are formed much closer to the parent plant. Many plants that grow in 'clumps' reproduce in this way. Some *Cryptocoryne* and *Echinodorus* species produce offsets, creating the appearance of a larger individual plant. Offsets can be gently removed from the main plant and replanted elsewhere in the aquarium once the roots have been trimmed. Separating offsets normally requires removing the whole plant from the tank first, so do not carry out this procedure too often, otherwise the parent plant may sustain lasting damage. When moving established plants, be sure to remove the entire rootstock from the substrate. Any root left behind will rot and could prevent plants from rooting in that area or adversely affect the health of nearby roots.

Propagating from adventitious plantlets

1 The plantlets underneath this leaf are well developed, while the 'mother' leaf is beginning to die back to allow the plantlets to drop off. This makes them easier to remove by hand and plant out separately.

2 The new plantlet is now large enough to be replanted. Simply pull it from the main leaf. As the 'mother' leaf is beginning to fall apart, remove it from the main plant and discard it. Otherwise, it will simply rot away.

Adventitious plantlets Small plantlets that form on various parts of an adult plant are described as adventitious plantlets. Depending on the species, these may form on the leaves, stem nodes or on shoots. Small leaves are produced first, followed by roots, and the new plant remains attached to the parent plant until the area of attachment dies back and the new plant is released. Once a plantlet has a few leaves and at least 3-4cm (1.2-1.6in) of root growth, it can be carefully removed from the parent plant and replanted. It is often best to leave the new plantlet to grow as much as possible before doing this. Common species of aquarium plants that can be propagated by plantlets include *Echinodorus, Microsorium, Aponogeton* and *Bolbitis*.

Propagating aquarium plants

Artificial aquarium propagation

Aquarium plants can also be propagated artificially by means of cuttings, and by dividing rhizomes and rootstocks.

Propagating from cuttings

Virtually all stem plants can be propagated by cuttings, taken from both the top and middle stem areas. Taking cuttings is also a good way of 'thickening' up plants, as side shoots are often produced from the main plant as a result of cutting.

Cuttings All plants with a central stem supporting a number of leaves can be propagated by cuttings. Most stem plants sold either as bunches or potted up are simply top cuttings from established plants. Cuttings can be taken from both the top and middle stem sections, as well as from side shoots. However, the top section of a stem plant includes the growing point and a top cutting is likely to establish more quickly than a cutting taken from other areas of the plant.

A normal stem will have a number of nodes (points at which leaves are produced) and these will also form roots if a cutting is taken. Using sharp scissors, take a cutting

1 *To take a top cutting, snip off a length of stem with several leaves or nodes. Cut between the nodes with sharp scissors. For the best results, take cuttings from the fastest growing and/or healthiest stem.*

2 *Strip away the leaves from one or two nodes at the base of the cutting to allow the plant to root more quickly. Roots will form from the stripped nodes. Make sure they are beneath the substrate when planting.*

3 *Push the cutting into the substrate so that the lower leaves are just resting on the substrate surface. Roots should grow from the base and the plant will establish quickly, although lower leaves may die off.*

just above a node, with at least four or five nodes above it. The bottom set of nodes on the cutting will be the area where new roots develop. Carefully remove the leaves on these nodes and plant the stem cutting in the substrate so that the stripped lower nodes are just covered by the substrate. The cutting will start to produce roots and once firmly anchored in the substrate, should start to grow and produce new leaves. The plant that 'supplied' the cutting should also continue to grow and may produce side shoots from the point where the cutting was taken. Since taking cuttings from parent plants or regular pruning encourages the production of side shoots, it can also be used as a method of creating a 'bushier' plant.

Rhizomes A rhizome is a modified stem that resembles a thick root at the base of the plant. It is often used as a storage organ, as well as for the production of new shoots. To get to it, you will need to remove the whole plant from the substrate, taking care not to damage the roots. To produce new plants, cut the rhizome with a sharp knife and divide it, ensuring that each division has at least one good shoot. If the original plant or any cuttings or divisions have a large amount of rootstock, trim this to about 2.5cm (1in) in length before replanting. Trimming the old roots will reduce the amount of damage caused by replanting and ensures that fresh, new roots develop quickly. Plants that root on rock and wood, such as *Microsorium* or *Anubias* species, can be propagated in this way. Using a length of cotton, tie the new divisions either to porous rock or to suitable pieces of bogwood until they have become firmly anchored.

Above: *The rhizome of an African fern* (Bolbitis heudelotii). *A new shoot to the right of the rhizome indicates that this is the growing end and the best area from which to take a cutting.*

Propagating aquarium plants

Dividing cryptocoryne

Cryptocorynes are good examples of plants that produce many offsets directly next to the parent plant.

1 *Start by removing the main plant from the substrate. Carry out this procedure with care to avoid any damage to the plant's roots.*

Division Plants that grow in clumps will either produce offsets or carry on producing leaves from the main rootstock. If a plant is large enough, you can divide the main root, creating two or more separate plants. Depending on the condition of the rootstock, either pull the plant apart gently or cut it with a sharp knife. Plant the divisions separately in the substrate and they should develop into healthy new plants.

3 *Once the plant has been divided, either by hand or using a sharp knife, trim the roots and replant the two sections into the aquarium.*

2 *Separate the leaves to establish the natural divisions within the plant. If the roots are relatively untangled, the plant can be separated by hand.*

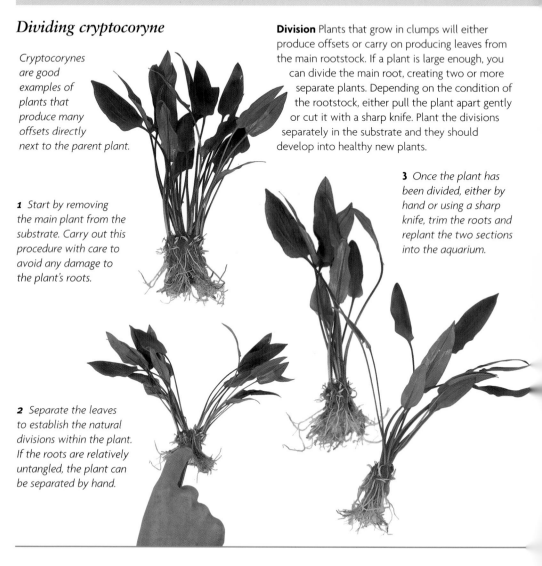

Dividing Java fern

Because Java fern is grown above the substrate, the rhizome is easy to see and division is relatively simple to carry out.

Below: *A good specimen can be divided into a number of plants. As they already have established roots, they should begin to grow almost immediately.*

Check the plant carefully before cutting so that you find the best places to separate the sections.

Above: *Cut the rhizome with a pair of sharp scissors. Each division should have at least two or three well-developed leaves, as well as a good root system.*

Trim the trailing roots before replanting.

Maintaining a planted aquarium

Most of the maintenance in a planted aquarium is concentrated on the plants themselves, which need trimming, separating and tidying up. If this is carried out continually, but in small amounts, a mature planted aquarium will need only minimal attention.

The substrate

A good substrate will look after itself for the most part but should not be left alone completely. Firstly, you should remove any organic debris resting on the surface of the substrate. This promotes bacterial problems in bottom-dwelling fish and may also clog fine-leaved plants, preventing light from reaching the leaves. Gently stirring the water above the substrate will cause the debris to rise higher into the water, where it can be taken up by filters. In an aquarium with a great deal of surface debris, this should be done at least three times a week, preferably more. Alternatively, surface debris can be siphoned away, but take care not to damage any plants in the process.

To avoid a build-up of anaerobic patches of substrate, gently disturb the substrate with your fingers every month or so, loosening the whole of the substrate, and creating gaps in it.

Over long periods of time, all substrates will lose their ability to hold one or more vital nutrients. This nutrient depletion can be countered by increasing other forms of fertilisation, such as liquid fertilisers. Nevertheless, there usually comes a point when it is best to replace the entire substrate in the aquarium. This process is highly disruptive and it is vital to handle all the plants with great care. Remove each one individually and trim all the roots before replanting them in the new substrate.

Above: *Use a siphon cleaner to remove organic debris from the substrate and to draw off any small plant trimmings. Carefully move the cleaner from side to side at substrate level.*

Left and below: *Remove the foam from an internal filter and squeeze it out in aquarium water in a bucket to retain the colony of beneficial bacteria. Remove any visible debris.*

Right: *By the time you have finished, the filter foam will look a lot cleaner. It is a good idea to replace half the filter foam when it shows signs of not returning to its original shape when squeezed.*

house the plants and fish in a separate aquarium with the water and filter from the original tank. Once the new substrate is in place, return the fish, plants, filter and mature water to the original aquarium. A normal substrate, high in organics, will need to be replaced after about three years of use.

Equipment

Clean out internal filters and the media in them at least twice a month. External filters should be cleaned at least once a month. Always clean any filtration media in water from the aquarium; never use tapwater, which may contain enough chlorine to kill beneficial bacteria. To ensure that any pumps remain in working order for as long as possible, be sure to clean both the impeller and the impeller housing.

If the light in the aquarium is provided by fluorescent tubes, replace these every 6-12 months, even if they appear to be working properly. The intensity of light from a fluorescent tube diminishes quickly and although a year-old tube may seem to be functioning correctly, its output will be less than half that of a new tube.

Clean condensation trays or cover-glasses every week to prevent the build-up of deposits, as these will also significantly reduce the amount of light reaching the plants (see page 41).

Normally, you can replace the substrate and replant the plants straight after, so simply store the plants in water from the aquarium while you replace the substrate. If the new substrate is to contain soil-like media, such as nutrient-rich substrates, you may need to strip the aquarium completely and add the substrate while the aquarium is empty. In this case,

Maintaining a planted aquarium

Water quality

It is important to check the levels of ammonia, nitrites, nitrates, pH and hardness in the aquarium on a regular basis. If possible, carry out these tests every week and keep a record of each one and the date it was performed. It is also possible to test for the presence of certain nutrients, but this only needs to be done when plants show signs of a deficiency or excess of nutrients. Keeping a record of test results is a good way of checking any trends in the aquarium, such as rises in nitrates or softening of the water over time. In most cases, regular water changes, using at least half tapwater, will keep the water in good condition. The frequency of water changes depends on the individual requirements of the aquarium. For most planted aquariums, a small (10-15%) water change every week or two should be sufficient. Remember that water changes do not only reduce toxins, but also replenish nutrients, so even if the water quality seems good, you should still carry out water changes.

Tapwater often contains high levels of chlorine, which will need to be removed before the water is added to the aquarium. There are many proprietary dechlorinators available for aquariums, but use these with care in a planted aquarium. Many water conditioners contain properties that remove metals from tapwater. Normally this is beneficial for both plants and fish, but many metals are also nutrients vital to plant health. Using metal-removing dechlorinators to condition water will not only remove useful nutrients from the new water, but also nutrients already present in the aquarium. There are various ways of preventing this. Firstly, if you use dechlorinators, stick to the simple products

Above: When taking a water sample, select a clean test vial from the kit and rinse it first in the aquarium. Washing in tapwater may distort the final test results.

Above: Tests usually involve starting with a 5 or 10ml water sample. For accurate results, the bottom of the meniscus must sit on the line printed on the vial.

Above: Adding the right amount of reagent is vital. Tablets contain a measured dose.

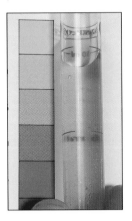

Above right: Nitrate levels can go quite high, especially in sparsely planted tanks where the plants do not use enough of it as food. This 25mg/litre result is typical and safe in most aquariums.

and avoid those with 'added benefits', such as metal removal, aloe-vera and 'conditioners'. Secondly, remember that water can be dechlorinated by aeration over a 24-hour period, without any need for chemical dechlorinators. Special 'pre-filter' units are also available that remove chlorine from tapwater, but these are expensive and often unjustified.

Over time, water in a planted aquarium may turn a slightly 'tea-yellow' colour as humic acids are released from organic material, particularly bogwood. The coloration has no effect on plants or fish and is not a sign of poor water conditions. However, you can remove the coloration using absorptive chemical media such as activated carbon. These types of filtration media should only be used for short periods, as they will also remove many useful nutrients (as well as medications) from the water.

The occasional use of chemical media in the planted aquarium may be valuable not just for removing water discoloration, but also to eliminate build-ups of unwanted metals and other chemicals. When using chemical media, do not carry out additional fertilisation (other than CO_2 fertilisation), as all the introduced nutrients will simply be taken out by the chemical media.

A flexible hose attached to the siphon takes water from the aquarium.

Right: *You can use a siphon cleaner to make a water change. Continue to siphon until you have reduced the water to the desired level. Aim to change 10-15% of the tank volume every week or two. Take care not siphon out any fish!*

Right: *Direct the water from the tank into a bucket on the ground. Siphon cleaners operate on the basis of removing lighter wastes while leaving the substrate relatively intact.*

Maintaining a planted aquarium

Keeping plants tidy

In a healthy planted aquarium with good lighting and balanced nutrients, the plants should grow and propagate at a relatively fast rate. If left unchecked, an attractive display can quickly become a tangled mass of vegetation. To keep plants looking their best, they will need to be regularly trimmed and/or older leaves must be removed to allow healthy, new ones to grow in their place.

Stem plants will often continue to grow until they reach the surface, at which point they either grow horizontally across the water or produce aerial leaves above it. Unless you want to encourage this growth habit, you should regularly trim the top portion of stem plants. When trimming plants, it is often better to take off a significant amount (say 10-15cm/4-6in) every other week, rather than small

Above: *Using sharp scissors, cut any dying leaves cleanly at the base of the stalk and remove them from the aquarium. Plants will continue to look their best if you maintain them regularly.*

Right: *Stem plants that reach the water surface can be trimmed with scissors. Remove larger portions as needed, rather than regularly cutting small trimmings.*

amounts two or three times a week, which could eventually damage the plants. Taking off a larger portion also allows you to replant the cutting as a separate plant if you wish (as shown on page 58). In any case, since the stem plant will eventually become 'worn out' from continual growth and trimming back, you should use at least some of these top cuttings to replace the original plant.

Above: Think about where to snip off a long shoot. This hygrophila needs trimming, and cutting just above a node will encourage the plant to produce new, bushy growth.

Plants that produce leaves from the base, rather than on stems, can also be trimmed to prevent the leaves from growing too large. Older leaves (normally the larger ones) can be carefully separated from the base and discarded, allowing new leaves to form in their place. Applied over a period of time, this method of trimming can be used to influence the eventual size of the plant. For example, if older leaves are regularly removed before they reach their full size, the plant will remain small and compact. However, if the plant is allowed to grow large leaves initially, it will continue to produce larger and taller leaves in succession, and the plant will eventually attain a substantial size.

As leaves age, they often become covered in algae or may begin to die off at the edges, sometimes developing dark patches or even holes. At this point they should be removed from the aquarium, because not only do they become unsightly, but they are often less useful to the plant than the new leaves that would grow in their place.

Plants do not have an unlimited lifespan; there comes a point when individual plants simply stop producing new leaves and will need to be replaced. When taking out old plants, it is very important to remove as much of the root as possible. Any root left in the substrate will rot and may create anaerobic conditions.

Left: Algae has affected this Monosolenium tenerum. *This can be removed by siphoning. It is vital to remove algae so that it cannot interfere with photosynthesis.*

Routine maintenance

Daily
- Check for any missing livestock and examine the health of all the fishes. Look for red marks on the body and gills, excess mucus, gasping or unusual behaviour.
- Check the water temperature.
- Check that filters and lights are working.

Twice weekly
- Gently disturb any fine-leaved plants, such as cabomba, and dense foreground species, such as hairgrass, to remove any trapped detritus, which can hinder photosynthesis.

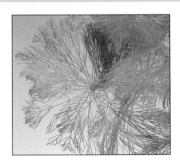

Above: *Keep fine-leaved plants such as* Limnophila *free of debris.*

Weekly
- Test the water for nitrites (NO_2), nitrates (NO_3), pH and hardness.
- Remove dead leaves and other plant matter.
- Siphon out or remove any organic debris from the top layer of substrate and replace the water removed during this process with new, dechlorinated water. This will also constitute a small water change, replacing minerals and helping to lower nitrates and phosphates.
- Replenish liquid fertilisers after water changes according to the maker's instructions.
- Using an algae magnet, pad or scraper, clean the inside front and side glass, even if little algae is present. This prevents a build-up of algae that can be hard to remove.
- If you have a condensation cover, wipe it clean to avoid a reduction in light penetration to the plants.

Above: *Using a scraper on the end of a handle is one method of removing algae and debris from the inside of the aquarium glass. Another strategy is to wipe the glass with a wad of filter wool (dispose of it afterwards). To save your hands getting wet, use an algae magnet on a string or one fitted with internal air pockets.*

Every two weeks
- Thoroughly clean half the sponge in the internal filter, using water from the aquarium. Then tip this water away.

Monthly
- Switch off external filters and clean the media in water from the aquarium. Then tip the water away.
- Replace any filter floss in an external filter.

Every three months

- Check the substrate for compaction and gently loosen it with your fingers.
- Remove and clean any impellers and impeller housings in pumps and filters.

Every 6-12 months

- If fluorescent tubes are the main source of lighting, replace them even if they are still working. After 10-12 months they will have lost much of their intensity.
- Replace filter sponges. Over time, the bacterial capacity of sponges will diminish and they need to be replaced. If sponges are the main biological medium, then replace half at a time, leaving a month in-between. This will reduce the loss of beneficial filter bacteria.

Above: Clean the internal filter, including the impeller and casing, using fresh filter wool. Remove plant fragments from the slots.

Above: To ensure maximum efficiency, replace fluorescent tubes, even if they are still working. To protect the tubes from moisture over the aquarium, waterproof endcaps are fitted on the flying leads.

When needed

- Replenish liquid or tablet fertilisers according to the maker's instructions. Establishing a good regime for introducing nutrients into the aquarium is vital for the continued health and growth of plants. However, the type and quantity of fertilisation will vary from one aquarium to another.
- Check and replenish any CO_2 supply systems that may be in use.
- Trim any tall stem plants, so that they do not grow across the surface and block out light to other plants. Replant the cuttings if you wish.
- If tall-stemmed plants are looking thin near the base, remove them, cut off the upper halves and replant.
- If the leaves of plants such as large Echinodorus sp. have grown too big, remove the outermost leaves and trim the roots slightly. The plant will respond by producing fresh, smaller leaves.
- Old plant leaves may become tattered or covered in algae. Remove them to prevent the spread of algae and to allow new leaves to grow.
- Over time, some plants will age and begin to look less healthy. They stop growing and become tattered. If this happens, remove and replace them. Be sure to take out the entire rootstock, as any pieces left over may rot and pollute the substrate.

Creating a display

The difference between a well-planted aquarium and a stunning display aquarium lies in good aquascaping. Creating a display is not simply a matter of placing plants and decor in the right combinations or in the right places, it means being imaginative – even inspired. There are certainly methods of planting and guidelines to positioning

that will help you create a good display aquarium, but ultimately, the design should be the realisation of your personal vision.

These days, aquarists are faced with a very wide range of rocks, wood and other decor, but not all materials are suitable for a planted aquarium. When making a choice, it is often best to keep things

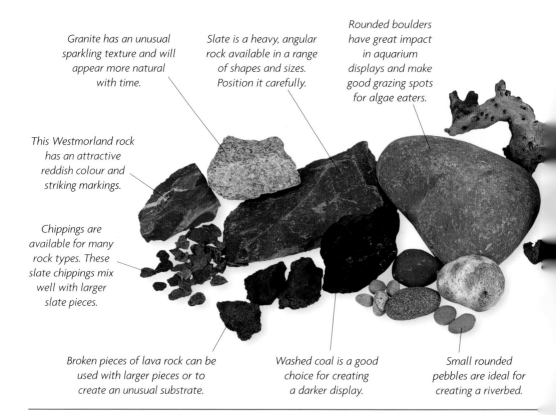

Granite has an unusual sparkling texture and will appear more natural with time.

Slate is a heavy, angular rock available in a range of shapes and sizes. Position it carefully.

Rounded boulders have great impact in aquarium displays and make good grazing spots for algae eaters.

This Westmorland rock has an attractive reddish colour and striking markings.

Chippings are available for many rock types. These slate chippings mix well with larger slate pieces.

Broken pieces of lava rock can be used with larger pieces or to create an unusual substrate.

Washed coal is a good choice for creating a darker display.

Small rounded pebbles are ideal for creating a riverbed.

simple and stick to, say, one or two types of rock, rather than crowd the aquarium with all manner of objects. All the decor should, of course, be bought and not collected from the wild. Clean it well before using it in the aquarium. This means soaking bogwood thoroughly to remove the tannins and scrubbing rocks to remove dust and debris.

Mopani bogwood is precleaned and has a rough dark side and a smooth paler side.

Twisted roots can be used to represent overhanging branches and tree roots.

Above: *To test if a rock is likely to alter water quality, simply pour on some acidic substance such as vinegar. If the rock contains any calcareous substances, it will begin to fizz gently. If there is no fizzing, the rock should be safe to use in a freshwater aquarium.*

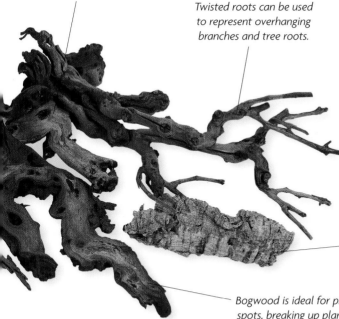

Cork bark is buoyant and will need to be weighted down or fixed in place. An ideal material for hiding tank equipment.

Bogwood is ideal for providing hiding spots, breaking up planted areas and representing fallen or dead vegetation.

Creating a display

Laying out a design

Providing you have access to a good range of materials, it is sometimes possible to design and create a good display on impulse, but results are often far better if you do some preplanning. Sketching out a rough design for the aquarium allows you to assess the number of plants you will need and check the practical aspects of the display. Taking an overhead view, make a sketch of the aquarium, showing all the filtration, heating and other equipment that will be present inside it and then divide the space into foreground, midground and background areas. This sketch then becomes the framework on which you can 'build up' the planting areas and position the decor.

When deciding where to site decor other than plants and designing the display as a whole, a good rule is to have one main focal point to attract

A planting plan for your aquarium

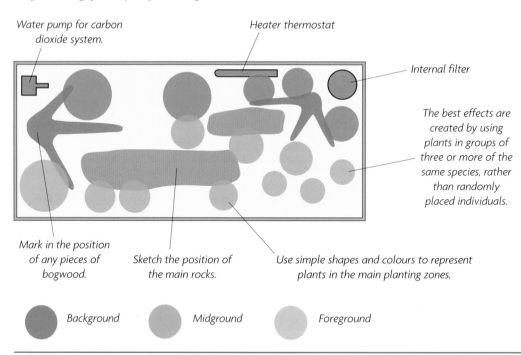

Water pump for carbon dioxide system.

Heater thermostat

Internal filter

The best effects are created by using plants in groups of three or more of the same species, rather than randomly placed individuals.

Mark in the position of any pieces of bogwood.

Sketch the position of the main rocks.

Use simple shapes and colours to represent plants in the main planting zones.

Background   Midground   Foreground

interest and, using similar decor, a second, smaller area to provide a 'counterbalance'. For example, you could complement a large, central group of cobbles and plants with a couple of smaller cobbles and plants elsewhere in the aquarium.

Grouping plants

Individual plant species all have a 'place' in the aquarium. Taller stem plants and large-leaved species work well as background plants, while smaller plants can be used in the midground, with low-growing species in the foreground. However, there are no set rules for what constitutes a

Above: *The completed display based on the planting plan. Do not be tempted to fill the aquarium with plants straightaway – leave room for growth.*

foreground or background plant and it is often better to mix up the areas a little. Generally speaking, a larger plant should be placed behind a smaller plant for obvious reasons, but plants can be grouped and placed in a number of different ways to create an interesting design. Although it is tempting to use many different species, it is often a lot easier and more effective to use a limited number of species in larger groupings.

Placing plants in the aquarium

BACKGROUND

Alternanthera reineckii
Ammannia gracilis
Anubias barteri var. barteri;
A. congensis
Aponogeton ulvaceus
Bacopa caroliniana
Barclaya longifolia
Blyxa echinosperma
Bolbitis heudelotii
Cabomba spp.
Ceratophyllum demersum
Ceratopteris cornuta
Crinum natans; C. thaianum
Cryptocoryne balansae;
C. undulata; C. wendtii
Echinodorus amazonicus;
E. bleheri; E. cordifolius;
E. grandiflorus; E. macrophyllus;
E. major; E. osiris; E. parviflorus;
E. uruguayensis
Egeria densa
Elodea canadensis
Eusteralis stellata
Gymnocoronis spilanthoides
Heteranthera zosterifolia
Hygrophila corymbosa;
H. difformis; H. guianensis;
H. polysperma
Limnophila aquatica;
L. sessiliflora
Ludwigia glandulosa;
L. repens; L. palustris
Microsorium pteropus
Myriophyllum spp.

Najas indica
Nesaea crassicaulis
Nuphar japonica
Nymphaea lotus
Potamogeton crispus
Rotala macrandra; R. rotundifolia
Sagittaria subulata
Shinnersia rivularis
Spathiphyllum wallisii
Vallisneria americana; V. asiatica
var. biwaensis; V. gigantea;
V. spiralis

MIDGROUND

Alternanthera reineckii
Ammannia gracilis
Anubias angustifolia 'Afzelii' ;
A. barteri var. barteri; A. gracilis;
A. lanceolata

Aponogeton boivinianus;
A. crispus; A. madagascariensis;
A. ulvaceus
Bacopa caroliniana; B. monnieri
Barclaya longifolia
Blyxa echinosperma; B. japonica
Bolbitis heudelotii
Cardamine lyrata
Ceratophyllum demersum
Cryptocoryne affinis; C. balansae;
C. beckettii; C. lutea;
C. pontederiifolia; C. undulata;
C. walkeri; C. wendtii
Didiplis diandra
Echinodorus amazonicus;
E. cordifolius; E. horemanii;
E. osiris; E. parviflorus;
E. uruguayensis
Egeria densa
Eichhornia azurea
Eleocharis acicularis; E. parvula;
E. vivipara
Eusteralis stellata
Fontinalis antipyretica
Gymnocoronis spilanthoides
Hemianthus micranthemoides
Heteranthera zosterifolia
Hydrocotyle leucocephala;
H. sibthorpioides; H. verticillata
Hygrophila corymbosa;

Ludwigia repens *grows up to
50cm (20in) tall and makes
an excellent background or
midground plant.*

H. guianensis
Lagarosiphon major
Limnophila sessiliflora
Lobelia cardinalis
Ludwigia repens; L. palustris
Lysimachia nummularia
Microsorium pteropus
Myriophyllum spp.
Najas indica
Nuphar japonica
Nymphaea lotus; N. stellata
Nymphoides aquatica
Potamogeton crispus
Rotala macrandra; R. rotundifolia
Sagittaria platyphylla; S. subulata
Saururus cernuus
Shinnersia rivularis
Spathiphyllum wallisii
Vallisneria americana; V. tortifolia

FOREGROUND

Anubias angustifolia 'Afzelii';
A. barteri var. nana; A. gracilis;
A. lanceolata
Aponogeton crispus;
A. madagascariensis; A. undulatus
Bacopa monnieri; B. rotundifolia
Blyxa japonica
Cardamine lyrata
Cryptocoryne affinis; C. balansae;
C. beckettii; C. lutea; C. parva;
C. pontederiifolia; C. undulata;
C. walkeri; C. willisii
Didiplis diandra
Echinodorus bolivianus;

E. tenellus
Eleocharis acicularis
Eusteralis stellata
Fontinalis antipyretica
Glossostigma elatinoides
Hemianthus callitrichoides
Heteranthera zosterifolia
Hydrocotyle leucocephala;
H. sibthorpioides; H. verticillata
Lagarosiphon major
Lilaeopsis novae-zelandiae
Lobelia cardinalis
Lysimachia nummularia
Marsilea hirsuta
Micranthemum umbrosum
Nymphoides aquatica
Sagittaria platyphylla; S. pusilla
Samolus valerandi
Saururus cernuus
Vallisneria tortifolia
Vesicularia dubyana

Above: The roots of Salvinia natans absorb nutrients from the water.

FLOATING

Azolla spp.
Ceratophyllum demersum
Ceratopteris cornuta
Cladophora aegagropila
Eichhornia crassipes
Hydrocotyle leucocephala
Limnobium laevigatum
Ludwigia helminthorrhiza
Micranthemum umbrosum
Monosolenium tenerum
Najas indica
Nymphoides aquatica
Pistia stratiotes
Riccia fluitans
Salvinia spp.
Trapa natans

Left: Marsilea hirsuta – an attractive foreground plant.

An open-topped aquarium

The water surface of an aquarium without a hood can be used as an extension of the display. Floating plants and leaves produced above the water add an extra element. If the aquarium is large enough, you can also include bogwood and houseplants. An open-topped aquarium must be illuminated with pendant-type lighting. If plants are to grow on or above the water surface, allow enough space (at least 45cm/18in) between the light and the water surface so that the leaves do not overheat. For the same reason, provide good ventilation. If the light source is very hot, it may be worth carefully positioning a small fan to create a cooling air current above the aquarium.

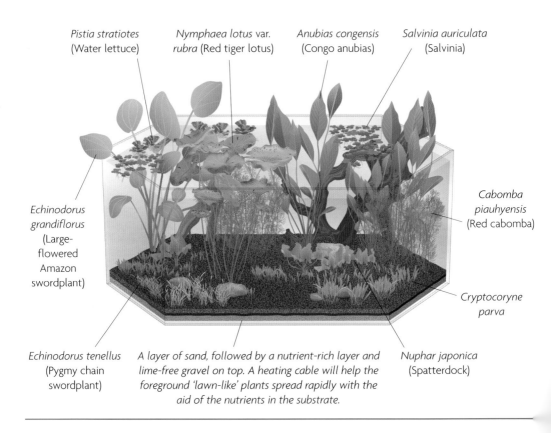

Pistia stratiotes (Water lettuce)

Nymphaea lotus var. *rubra* (Red tiger lotus)

Anubias congensis (Congo anubias)

Salvinia auriculata (Salvinia)

Echinodorus grandiflorus (Large-flowered Amazon swordplant)

Cabomba piauhyensis (Red cabomba)

Cryptocoryne parva

Echinodorus tenellus (Pygmy chain swordplant)

A layer of sand, followed by a nutrient-rich layer and lime-free gravel on top. A heating cable will help the foreground 'lawn-like' plants spread rapidly with the aid of the nutrients in the substrate.

Nuphar japonica (Spatterdock)

Plant list

1. *Anubias congensis* (Congo anubias)
2. *Cabomba piauhyensis* (Red cabomba)
3. *Cryptocoryne parva*
4. *Echinodorus grandiflorus* (Large-flowered Amazon swordplant)
5. *Echinodorus tenellus* (Pygmy chain swordplant)
6. *Nuphar japonica* (Spatterdock)
7. *Nymphaea lotus var. rubra* (Red tiger lotus)

Floating plants

Pistia stratiotes (Water lettuce)
Salvinia auriculata (Salvinia)

Suitable fish

*Choose surface-dwelling fish for movement when seen from above. Floating plants and tiger lotus leaves provide cover for hatchetfish (*Carnegiella, Gasteropelecus and Thoracocharax spp.), livebearers and gouramis. Small algae-eating fish, such as Otocinclus, will browse on the leaves of Echinodorus tenellus. (Larger algae eaters may damage the thin tiger lotus leaves.) Small corydoras catfish will remove debris from the smaller-leaved foreground plants. Tetras and small rasboras make good shoaling groups amongst the vegetation. For a more 'showy' effect, choose larger fish, such as angelfish.*

Left: *Hatchetfish swim just below the water surface looking for food. They appreciate surface plant cover.*

Right: *Angelfish (*Pterophyllum scalare*) make a strong impact, but may pick off small tankmates.*

A low-light aquarium

As we have seen, the correct lighting is vital for the continued growth and health of aquarium plants, but in some situations, providing suitably intense light may be costly or impractical. Luckily for the aquarist, there are plants that thrive in shady streams with little natural light, and these have adapted to grow in relatively dim conditions. Indeed, some of them will not do well if given too much light in the aquarium.

One limitation of low light conditions is that suitable foreground plants are hard to obtain. Because foreground plants are low growing, they do not receive as much light as taller plants nearer the water surface. This means that most foreground plants require a more intense light source in the aquarium. The exceptions to this rule are many *Cryptocoryne* species, which come from shallow streams, often shaded by terrestrial vegetation.

Salvinia auriculata (Salvinia). Floating plants cast welcome shade on the plants beneath them.

Egeria densa (Elodea)

Hygrophila corymbosa

Ceratophyllum demersum (Hornwort)

Microsorium pteropus (Java fern)

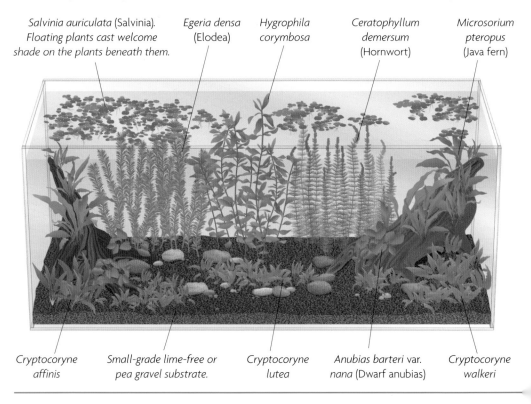

Cryptocoryne affinis

Small-grade lime-free or pea gravel substrate.

Cryptocoryne lutea

Anubias barteri var. *nana* (Dwarf anubias)

Cryptocoryne walkeri

Many slow-growing plants, such as Java fern *(Microsorium pteropus)* or *Anubias* sp., can be kept in low-light conditions. Slow-growing plants generally have a slow metabolism, so they have less need of light energy. The plants in this display can be kept in a tank with one or two fluorescent tubes.

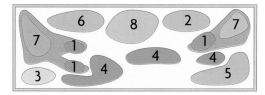

Plant list

1. *Anubias barteri* var. *nana* (Dwarf anubias)
2. *Ceratophyllum demersum* (Hornwort)
3. *Cryptocoryne affinis*
4. *Cryptocoryne lutea*
5. *Cryptocoryne walkeri*
6. *Egeria densa* (Elodea)
7. *Microsorium pteropus* (Java fern)
8. *Hygrophila corymbosa*

Floating plant

Salvinia auriculata (Salvinia)

Suitable fish

The smaller cryptocorynes should be kept free from algae and debris, so small algae eaters, such as Otocinclus spp., and scavengers, such as Corydoras spp., are fine. All the plants used here are quite hardy, so slightly boisterous fish can be added, such as barbs and danios. These fish will also appreciate the open swimming space in the centre of the aquarium. Barbs, including the tiger barb (Barbus tetrazona), golden barb (B. semifasciolatus), rosy barb (B. conchonius), black ruby barb (B. nigrofasciatus) and cherry barb (B. titteya), are all suitable.

Above: *The vivid cherry barbs enjoy the cover provided by dense planting, as well as the shade of floating plants.*

Left: *Perched on plant leaves or up against the glass, otocinclus catfish rasp constantly on algae growth.*

A hardwater aquarium

Depending on where you live, your water may be hard and alkaline (high pH). Although it is possible to remove hardness and soften water with proprietary chemicals and filtration systems, it can be costly and time consuming. Most plants do best in medium-soft water and although many will acclimatise to harder water for short periods, in the long-term, hard water will damage them and adversely affect their growth. However, there are hardwater areas in the wild where plants thrive, and the importance of soft water in planted aquariums is debatable as far as these species are concerned. A few plants survive notably better in harder water; a typical example is elodea or pondweed *(Egeria densa)*. Adding CO_2 fertilisation in hardwater conditions is an excellent idea, as it will slightly acidify the water and compensate for the drop in available nutrients (see pages 52-53).

Vallisneria asiatica var. *biwaensis* (Corkscrew vallisneria)   *Hygrophila stricta* (Thai stricta)   *Cardamine lyrata* (Chinese ivy)   *Cabomba caroliniana* (Green cabomba)

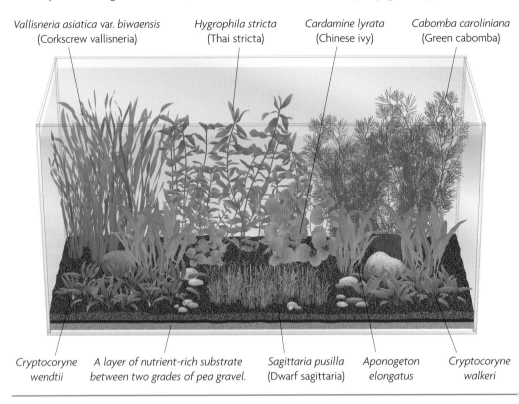

Cryptocoryne wendtii   *A layer of nutrient-rich substrate between two grades of pea gravel.*   *Sagittaria pusilla* (Dwarf sagittaria)   *Aponogeton elongatus*   *Cryptocoryne walkeri*

Plant list

1. *Aponogeton elongatus* (Elongated swordplant)
2. *Cabomba caroliniana* (Green cabomba)
3. *Cardamine lyrata* (Chinese ivy)
4. *Cryptocoryne walkeri*
5. *Cryptocoryne wendtii*
6. *Hygrophila stricta* (Thai stricta)
7. *Sagittaria pusilla* (Dwarf sagittaria)
8. *Vallisneria asiatica var. biwaensis* (Corkscrew vallisneria)

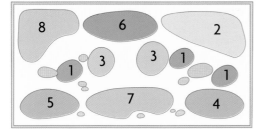

Above: *The active sailfin mollies patrol the middle to upper layers of the aquarium. The male (above) uses his dorsal fin to show off to the female.*

Below: *Zebra danios are very lively schooling fish that swim at all levels and prefer a well-planted aquarium in which they can dart from cover to cover.*

Suitable fish

Small, shoaling fish are ideal, although many tetras prefer softer water. Try danios, barbs and some rasboras instead. Corydoras are useful for removing debris. Algae eaters, such as Siamese flying foxes, Chinese hillstream loach and the sucking loach, do well in harder water. Consider midwater shoaling fish, including White Cloud Mountain minnows, zebra danios and giant danios. Many livebearers are also suited to this type of aquarium and to harder water. Common livebearers such as guppies, sailfin mollies, mollies, platies and swordtails are all ideal additions to this aquarium setup and easy to keep.

An African pool

Two main styles of aquarium can be recreated here. The fast, open waters of the Zaire River, for example, are home to few plants, since the high oxygen levels and rapid waters make conditions unsuitable for many species. This type of display would resemble a mountain stream biotope. By contrast, the lowland swamps, pools and slow-moving streams found in many places, often by the sides of faster-moving waters, are filled with aquatic plants. Along the muddy banks, species of *Azolla*, *Eleocharis acicularis* and *Ceratopteris* grow in dense clumps in the nutrient-rich water and substrate. Temperatures in these areas can approach 30°C (86°F), although these need not be recreated in the home aquarium. For best results, provide soft water with a pH between 6 and 6.8.

Crinum natans (African onion plant) *needs plenty of space, as it quickly grows upwards and along the surface.*

Barclaya longifolia (Orchid lily) *will add a little colour to the aquarium display.*

Lagarosiphon major (African waterweed) *grows quickly, assimilating nutrients from the water.*

Ammannia gracilis (Delicate ammannia). *Bright light intensifies the leaf colour.*

A darker top layer of pea gravel or lime-free substrate enhances the colour of plants and fish.

Bacopa monnieri (Dwarf bacopa) *grows short in open areas with bright light.*

Anubias barteri var. *nana.*

Place Bolbitis heudelotii (African fern) *near the top.*

This aquarium represents the deeper area of a pool. The lack of water movement and large fish makes it a suitable environment for delicate-leaved species, such as *Ammannia* and *Barclaya* spp. The broken branches and wood often found in these pools can be represented by bogwood, which also releases tannic acids, helping to keep the pH level low. Many of the plants used here may need good lighting and a supply of liquid fertiliser.

Suitable fish

The waterways of Africa are home to many species of fish, including a large number of characins. This display has a large, open area towards the front, which is ideal for active, shoaling fish such as the Congo tetra. Many catfish also come from African regions, including many of the Synodontis group, but some grow too large for a well-planted aquarium. Smaller catfish will enjoy the hiding places provided by the bogwood. Active, open-water-swimming catfish, such as the African glass catfish, can be kept in shoals. Larger midwater swimmers, such as many anabantids, are also suitable. Many killifishes also originate from African pools, although there are too many similar varieties to pick individual fish, and availability can be scarce.

Plant list

1. *Anubias barteri* var. *nana*
2. *Ammannia gracilis* (Delicate ammannia)
3. *Bacopa monnieri* (Dwarf bacopa)
4. *Barclaya longifolia* (Orchid lily)
5. *Bolbitis heudelotii* (African fern)
6. *Crinum natans* (African onion plant)
7. *Lagarosiphon major* (African waterweed)

Right: *Congo tetras appreciate surface cover and relatively dense planting, but may nibble fine-leaved species.*

Above: *In soft water with a pH level no higher than 7.5, killifish will reward you with stunning displays of colour.*

83

An Indonesian stream

In the rainforests of Indonesia there are many small tropical streams, often slow moving and swamplike, with overhanging vegetation creating light and dark patches. A number of aquatic plants flourish in the iron-rich reddish substrate, which is interspersed with small pebbles and stones. Many of the species for this biotope are slow growing and do not require strong light, making this setup an ideal one for beginners to attempt. However, not all the plants from this region will do well without strong lighting. Many are found in areas with little overhanging vegetation, where intense sunlight penetrates the shallow waters.

The red substrate often found in these types of streams is the result of iron, and can be recreated using a reddish brown gravel. Water quality should be neutral to soft (pH 6.8-7.2), with a temperature of 25-27°C (77-80°F). Provide additional CO_2.

Blyxa echinosperma
(Giant Japanese rush)

Hygrophila corymbosa
'Crispa'

Rotala wallichii
(Whorly rotala)

Rotala
rotundifolia

Microsorium
pteropus (Java fern)

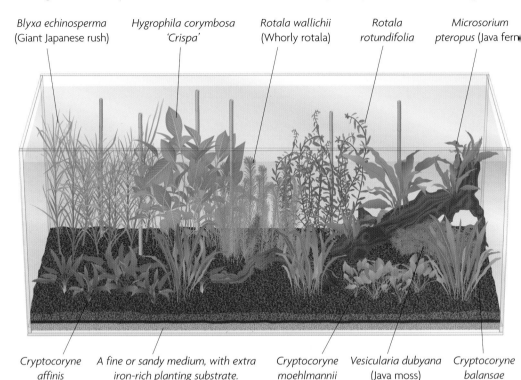

Cryptocoryne
affinis

A fine or sandy medium, with extra
iron-rich planting substrate.

Cryptocoryne
moehlmannii

Vesicularia dubyana
(Java moss)

Cryptocoryne
balansae

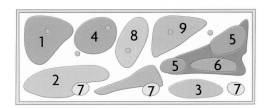

Plant list

1. *Blyxa echinosperma* (Giant Japanese rush)
2. *Cryptocoryne affinis*
3. *Cryptocoryne moehlmannii* (Moehlmann's cryptocoryne)
4. *Hygrophila corymbosa 'Crispa'*
5. *Microsorium pteropus* (Java fern)
6. *Vesicularia dubyana* (Java moss)
7. *Cryptocoryne balansae*
8. *Rotala wallichii* (Whorly rotala)
9. *Rotala rotundifolia*

Suitable fish

Many aquarium fish come from the Indonesian region, including some loaches, anabantids (gouramis), and barbs. Bottom dwellers for this aquarium include clown, horse-face and kuhli loaches, and algae eaters, such as the flying fox. For midwater swimmers, try tiger, checkered, five-banded or cherry barbs, and dwarf, harlequin or scissortail rasboras. Some gouramis are also suitable and will do well in the hiding places provided by the plants and bamboo. Suitable anabantids include Siamese fighting fish, three-spot, opaline and gold gouramis, pearl or chocolate gourami, paradisefish and the kissing gourami.

Left: Pearl gouramis prefer to occupy the upper layers of the tank and enjoy the shelter of reasonably dense planting.

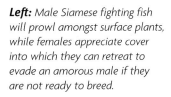

Left: Male Siamese fighting fish will prowl amongst surface plants, while females appreciate cover into which they can retreat to evade an amorous male if they are not ready to breed.

A mountain stream

The mountain streams found at the source of many rivers are inhospitable places for aquatic plants. Fast-moving water constantly batters the leaves and removes useful nutrients, while high oxygen levels make life hard for many plants. However, a few are highly adaptable and, although sparse, are readily found in such environments. To imitate this biotope, use large, rounded gravel for the top layer of the aquarium substrate, plus a number of cobbles or rocks. Overpowered filtration or additional pumps will recreate the fast-flowing water.

CO_2 fertilisation systems would be ineffective in this type of aquarium, as the increased air/water exchange would remove much of the CO_2 as soon as it was introduced. Instead, use liquid fertilisers to replace any substrate fertilisation. Water quality is relatively unimportant to both fishes and plants in this biotope. Recreating this type of environment in the aquarium results in a poor environment for most aquatic plants, but providing you choose the correct group of plants, you can be successful and achieve dramatic results.

Microsorium pteropus (Java fern)   *Fontinalis antipyretica* (Willow moss)   *Bolbitis heudelotii* (African fern)   *Vallisneria gigantea* (Giant vallisneria)

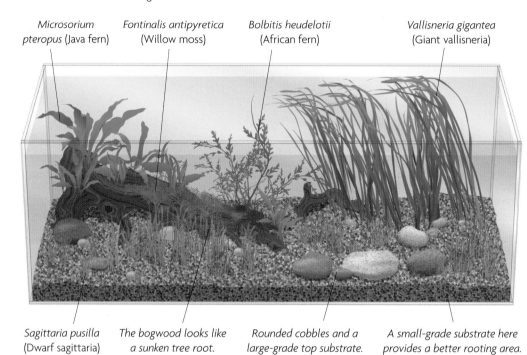

Sagittaria pusilla (Dwarf sagittaria)   *The bogwood looks like a sunken tree root.*   *Rounded cobbles and a large-grade top substrate.*   *A small-grade substrate here provides a better rooting area.*

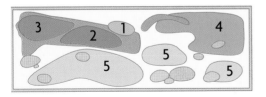

Plant list

1. *Bolbitis heudelotii* (African fern)
2. *Fontinalis antipyretica* (Willow moss)
3. *Microsorium pteropus* (Java fern)
4. *Vallisneria gigantea* (Giant vallisneria)
5. *Sagittaria pusilla* (Dwarf sagittaria)

Below: Synodontis nigriventris *routinely swims upside-down, hence its common name of upside-down catfish.*

Suitable fish

The fast-flowing nature of the aquarium can be enhanced by the use of fast-moving, active fish species. Many aquarium fish are well suited to this type of display although only a few are found in similar habitats in nature. Others simply come from river systems that may be fast flowing or from lowland streams. Fish with a 'streamlined' torpedo body shape (long and thin) are often from fast-flowing areas, as are algae eaters with flat, compressed bodies. Midwater swimmers include

Left: *White Cloud Mountain minnows are happiest when kept in shoals. Lone fish often become timid and lose their colour.*

White Cloud Mountain minnows, zebra and leopard danios, pearl danios, giant danios, glass catfish and silver-tipped tetras. Some smaller catfish will also do well in this aquarium; a few interesting varieties include the striped talking catfish, royal panaque, upside-down catfish and any of the shoaling Corydoras spp., which make ideal aquarium subjects.

PART TWO

A selection of aquarium plants

Aquarists are lucky in that there are literally hundreds of plant species suitable for aquarium conditions. Not all these plants are found in nature; many are cultivated varieties and as a result of crossbreeding and selective propagation, we can now choose from a wide range of plants with varied and interesting leaf shapes, colours, growth patterns and care requirements. Many plants also have subspecies, which are usually slightly different in height or leaf shape. Whatever type of aquarium design you are aiming for, there will be a good choice of plants to suit those conditions. Most aquatic outlets stock a good selection of aquarium plants, but if you are having difficulty obtaining a particular species, you may find that one of the many mail-order suppliers will stock it, or something similar. Whichever method you use to obtain plants, you should never be short of choices.

Although welcome, this wide selection of aquarium plants can be quite daunting. Where do you start?

We have looked at using plants in various areas of the tank: background, midground, foreground, etc. However, there are many other ways of grouping plants and drawing up a 'short list' of suitable species by a process of elimination. For example, plants can be selected for suitability by their height, spread, lighting and nutrient requirements, temperature as well as by location in the aquarium. A welcome challenge for aquarists is a biotope aquarium, where the fish and plants featured represent a natural habitat. In this case, plants can be chosen by their geographical origin. Or you can simply choose plants based on their colours, size and leaf shapes. However, a planted aquarium is not a static display and over time, plants can be moved around, swapped about, trimmed, propagated or removed as required.

In this part of the book over 150 plants are featured, along with descriptions of their environmental requirements, growth patterns, origins, and recommended locations.

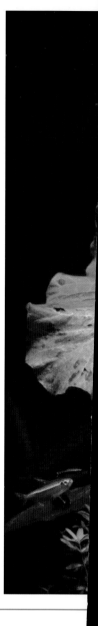

ALTERNANTHERA • AMMANNIA

Alternanthera reineckii

This red-leaved stem plant can be found in many different leaf forms and shades of colour. The top leaf surface may vary from olive-green to brown, while the underside is pink-red. A good source of iron will help to intensify the red colour. The plant is easy to care for if given the right conditions, which include strong lighting and a good iron-rich substrate. In larger aquariums, plant *A. reineckii* in small, well-spaced groups around the centre of the aquarium. The red leaves make it a good contrasting and focal specimen.

Difficulty Guide
1 Suitable for beginners.
2 Hardy and adaptable.
3 More challenging.
4 Difficult to care for and propagate.

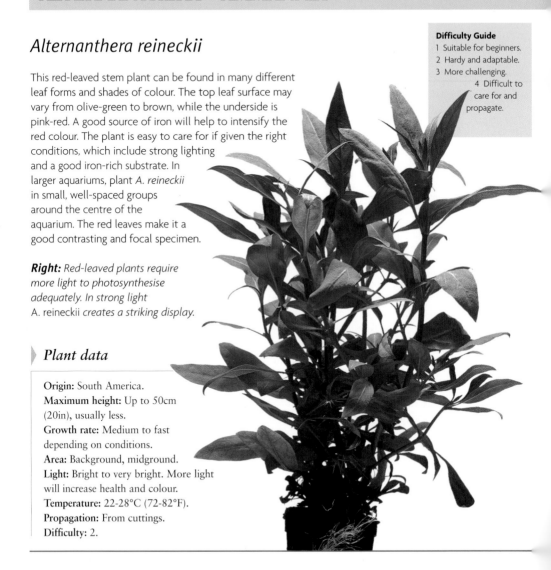

Right: *Red-leaved plants require more light to photosynthesise adequately. In strong light* A. reineckii *creates a striking display.*

Plant data

Origin: South America.
Maximum height: Up to 50cm (20in), usually less.
Growth rate: Medium to fast depending on conditions.
Area: Background, midground.
Light: Bright to very bright. More light will increase health and colour.
Temperature: 22-28°C (72-82°F).
Propagation: From cuttings.
Difficulty: 2.

Above: *The brownish red coloration of* Ammannia gracilis *provides an attractive contrast with the green of other aquarium plants.*

Ammannia gracilis
Delicate ammannia, Red ammannia

With its unusual leaf shape, *Ammannia gracilis* can look very effective when planted in groups and set against other plants with light green leaves. For the best effect, use shorter foreground plants around the base. The leaves vary in length depending on aquarium conditions. In good conditions, they may reach 10-12cm (4-4.7in) long, but 8-10cm (3.2-4in) is more usual. For the best results, provide bright lighting and a nutrient- and iron-rich, loose substrate. Under moderate lighting, the leaves may appear thin and/or weak. Bright lighting intensifies the leaf colour.

Plant data

Origin: Africa
Maximum height: 25-50cm (10-20in).
Growth rate: Medium to fast, depending on conditions.
Area: Background, midground.
Light: Very bright.
Temperature: 22-28°C (72-82°F)
Propagation: From cuttings and side shoots.
Difficulty: 2, 3.

ANUBIAS

ANUBIAS PLANTS
are a highly robust, undemanding and adaptable group that can be used in a number of ways in the aquarium. The plants come from various river and stream areas in Africa and are usually found on the edges of waterways and in marsh conditions. They have an adapted rhizome and roots that will attach to solid objects, such as wood or rocks, so substrate conditions are unimportant. With the minor exception of Anubias gracilis, *lighting is unimportant; indeed, bright lighting may even slow plant growth. In open-topped aquariums, anubias can be grown out of water, providing the root is either submerged or in very wet conditions. This makes it ideal for use in bog aquariums or paludariums. Some anubias will produce flowers and fruit on long stalks.*

Above: Anubias *sp. can be planted on rocks, wood, or in the substrate but the rhizome (the thicker root) must be in open water, otherwise it may die.*

Anubias angustifolia 'Afzelii'
Narrow-leaved anubias, Small anubias

This anubias is often sold as *A. barteri* var. *angustifolia* and *A. afzelii*, although *A. afzelii* is taller. The elongated leaves resemble those of *A. lanceolata*, which has slightly longer leaves and grows to about 25-30cm (10-12in). This attractive, thick-leaved plant is tough and adaptable and suitable for aquariums with boisterous or herbivorous fish.

This plant can be used in tanks with boisterous or herbivorous fish, which usually ignore it.

This attractive plant is not difficult to grow.

▶ *Plant data*

Origin: West Africa.
Maximum height: 20cm (8in).
Growth rate: Slow.
Area: Foreground, midground.
Light: Moderate.
Temperature: 20-28°C (68-82°F).
Propagation: Division, side shoots.
Difficulty: 1, 2.

Difficulty Guide
1 Suitable for beginners.
2 Hardy and adaptable.
3 More challenging.
4 Difficult to care for and propagate.

93

ANUBIAS

Anubias barteri var. barteri
Broadleaved anubias

This common *Anubias* species is an adaptable and robust plant that can be used in a number of ways in the aquarium. The main root, or rhizome, must be placed above the substrate, preferably attached to rock or bogwood, otherwise it may break down and die. As long as water is available to the root, the plant will grow above water or in bog conditions. The leaves of the broadleaved anubias are thick and sturdy and will survive the attentions of large, boisterous or herbivorous fish. The plant will live in a wide range of lighting conditions, but in brighter light the leaves are more compact and new leaves grow more quickly.

Below: *In a shady spot, the leaves of this and other* Anubias *species will not become covered with algae growth.*

Plant data

Origin: West Africa.
Maximum height: 30cm (12in).
Growth rate: Slow.
Area: Background, midground, or as a feature plant in the display.
Light: All light conditions.
Temperature: 22-28°C (72-82°F).
Propagation: From side shoots or by dividing the rhizome.
Difficulty: 1.

This low-growing variety of anubias will slowly attain a height of 15-25cm (6-10in), making it is suitable for both large and small aquariums.

Left: Anubias barteri *'Coffeefolia'* is a cultivated variety of Anubias, *with highly ridged, or 'crinkled', leaves. Young leaves are often reddish brown in colour, turning dark green later.*

Right: Anubias barteri *var.* caladiifolia '1705' *is very hardy and adaptable and well suited to most aquariums. The plant is very slow growing, but the leaves do not die easily, so given time, this plant can become quite large – up to 30cm (12in) or more.*

ANUBIAS

Anubias barteri var. nana
Dwarf anubias

This is one of the smallest *Anubias* species and makes an ideal foreground plant. The leaves are dark green, robust both physically and in appearance, and grow to about 8cm (3.2in) on the end of short stems. The plant will produce side shoots and grow horizontally, producing stems and leaves from a central root, or rhizome. It is adaptable, sturdy and well suited to any aquarium. This and other *Anubias* species can be grown on rocks and wood.

▸ Plant data

Origin: West Africa.
Maximum height: 12cm (4.7in).
Growth rate: Slow.
Area: Foreground, Specimen or unusual.
Light: Undemanding.
Temperature: 22-28°C (72-82°F).
Propagation: From side shoots or by dividing the rhizome.
Difficulty: 1.

Dwarf anubias flowers frequently in the aquarium.

Difficulty Guide
1 Suitable for beginners.
2 Hardy and adaptable.
3 More challenging.
4 Difficult to care for and propagate.

Anubias gracilis

The spade-shaped 8-12cm (3.2-4.7in) leaves and longer stalks give this anubias a much tidier appearance than smaller anubias, which may grow in seemingly random directions, but it is harder to care for than other anubias species. This plant does best when allowed to grow above the water surface and given plenty of nutrients. The substrate should be fairly loose and contain iron-rich fertiliser. In good conditions, this is an attractive and dominant plant that makes an excellent addition to any planted aquarium. For the best effect, give it plenty of room amongst smaller foreground plants.

Anubias congensis
Congo anubias

This adaptable and undemanding anubias from West Africa has become more widely available in recent years. It will grow quite tall, so is best suited to the background of the aquarium. The thick, leathery leaves are terrestrial in appearance. The Congo anubias can be used in bog or marsh conditions or in an open-topped aquarium, where it may produce leaves above the surface.

▶ *Plant data*

Origin: Africa.
Maximum height: 25-30cm (10-12in).
Growth rate: Slow, medium.
Area: Midground, foreground, or as feature plant in the display.
Light: Moderate or bright.
Temperature: 22-26°C (72-79°F).
Propagation: By rhizome division.
Difficulty: 2, 3.

APONOGETON

THE APONOGETONS *are a group of more than 40 species from Africa, Asia and Australia. The plants are found both in fully aquatic and terrestrial forms, as marsh or bog plants. In nature, many aponogetons occur in specialised habitats, which limits the number of plants suited to the broad-based conditions of the aquarium. However, about 15 varieties are suitable and around half of these are readily available. Many aponogetons are found in shallow bog or marginal areas that dry up annually. The plants found in these areas have a 'growth' period that coincides with natural rainy seasons and a 'rest' period during dry seasons. In the aquarium, these plants may grow well for a number of months and follow this with a period of little or no growth. Normally, growth is resumed if conditions are adequate. Conditions for good growth vary with individual plants, but a fine, nutrient-rich, warm substrate will benefit all aponogetons. Some varieties do well in harder water, while others need soft water. Most will produce stalks with flowers and produce fruit in the aquarium.*

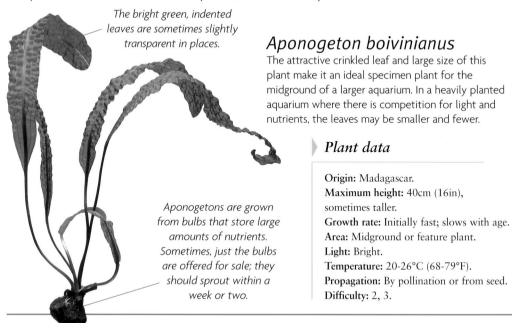

The bright green, indented leaves are sometimes slightly transparent in places.

Aponogetons are grown from bulbs that store large amounts of nutrients. Sometimes, just the bulbs are offered for sale; they should sprout within a week or two.

Aponogeton boivinianus

The attractive crinkled leaf and large size of this plant make it an ideal specimen plant for the midground of a larger aquarium. In a heavily planted aquarium where there is competition for light and nutrients, the leaves may be smaller and fewer.

▶ Plant data

Origin: Madagascar.
Maximum height: 40cm (16in), sometimes taller.
Growth rate: Initially fast; slows with age.
Area: Midground or feature plant.
Light: Bright.
Temperature: 20-26°C (68-79°F).
Propagation: By pollination or from seed.
Difficulty: 2, 3.

Aponogeton crispus
Crinkled or ruffled aponogeton

This popular, attractive and adaptable plant is readily available in the aquarium trade. Once settled into an aquarium and given all the right growing conditions, it will grow quickly, producing numerous olive green-brown ruffled leaves. These are normally up to 4cm (1.6in) wide and 20-35cm (8-14in) long. In weak light, the leaves are produced on longer stems that may spread across the water surface in search of more illumination. *A. crispus* may flower in the aquarium.

Many aponogetons have delicate-looking leaves. A source of nutrients in the substrate will help to keep them in good condition.

Plant data

Origin: Sri Lanka.
Maximum height: 35cm (14in), sometimes taller.
Growth rate: A period of strong growth, followed by very slow growth.
Area: Midground, foreground, or as a specimen feature plant.
Light: Bright.
Temperature: 22-30°C (72-86°F).
Propagation: By pollination or from seed.
Difficulty: 1, 2.

Difficulty Guide
1 Suitable for beginners.
2 Hardy and adaptable.
3 More challenging.
4 Difficult to care for and propagate.

APONOGETON

Aponogeton madagascariensis
Madagascan lace plant, Laceleaf

The laceleaf has become a popular aquarium plant, mainly due to its novel 'skeleton-like' appearance. This is due to a lack of leaf tissue; only the interconnecting veins are visible. It is not an easy plant to care for and requires clean and clear water conditions. Any algae or debris will clog the leaves and undermine the health of the plant. Be sure to keep it in soft water with a pH of 7 or lower. Narrow and wider leaf varieties are also available.

▶ Plant data

Origin: Madagascar.
Maximum height: Up to 65cm (25in).
Growth rate: Medium.
Area: Midground, foreground, or as a feature plant.
Light: Will do well in most conditions. Provide shade in well-lit aquariums.
Temperature: 20-22°C (68-72°F).
Propagation: From seed.
Difficulty: 3, 4.

Difficulty Guide
1 Suitable for beginners.
2 Hardy and adaptable.
3 More challenging.
4 Difficult to care for and propagate.

Water movement in the aquarium will help to keep these extraordinary leaves clear of debris.

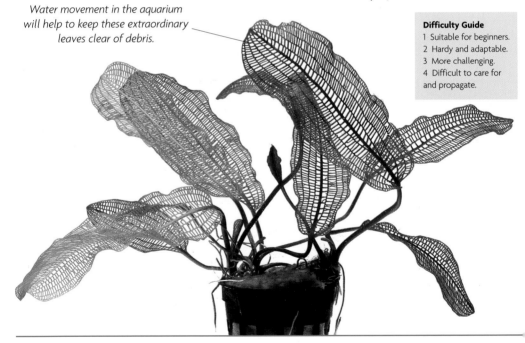

The highly ruffled leaves may vary in colour and sometimes appear pale green-yellow. This is natural and does not indicate a nutrient deficiency.

Aponogeton ulvaceus
Compact aponogeton

This aponogeton sports the common wavy-edged leaves of the genus, although the light green 4-6cm (1.6-2.4in)-wide leaves often appear smooth, shiny and slightly fleshy. The plant often grows in 'spurts', producing numerous new leaves before slowing down and eventually shedding the old ones. In bright light, it will grow taller.

Plant data

Origin: Sri Lanka.
Maximum height: 35-40cm (14-16in).
Growth rate: Medium.
Area: Background, midground, or as a specimen feature plant in the display.
Light: Moderate to bright.
Temperature: 22-28°C (72-82°C).
Propagation: From seed.
Difficulty: 2, 3.

Aponogeton undulatus

The long, thin shape of the leaf of this aponogeton from India makes it ideal for the midground of the aquarium, planted amongst other, smaller plants. The wavy edges of the leaf vary in complexity depending on the amount of light received by the plant. Can be kept in harder water.

AZOLLA • BACOPA

Azolla caroliniana
Water velvet

Water velvet is a small (2-3cm/0.8-1.2in diameter) floating plant that can be used in tropical and unheated aquariums and even in outdoor ponds (although in ponds it may die back in winter). In good conditions, the plant will spread rapidly and may need to be thinned regularly. It does not produce trailing roots, but will provide cover for some fishes. In brighter lighting, the plant sports an attractive 'rusty' red coloration. Provide adequate ventilation in the aquarium to prevent condensation on the leaves or overheating.

Plant data

Origin: North America.
Growth rate: Fast.
Area: Floating.
Light: Moderate to bright.
Temperature: 18-24°C (64-75°F).
Propagation: By division.
Difficulty: 1.

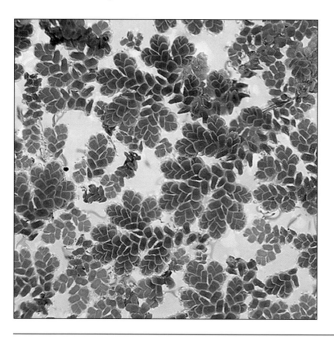

Azolla filiculoides
Azolla, Moss fern

This attractive and popular floating plant from America and Asia will do well in most aquariums, providing adequate ventilation is provided. The leaves vary in colour from a light green to a rusty red-brown, depending on conditions. Natural sunlight causes the leaves to turn red.

Left: *The small leaves of Azolla sp. have a velvety appearance, as a result of the many fine hairs that help to resist water and keep the plant afloat.*

Bacopa caroliniana
Giant bacopa

Given good lighting, a fine substrate and regular fertilisation, this plant will prove a highly adaptable and hardy variety, ideal for most aquariums. It does better in clean, clear water. The small (2.5cm/1in) pale-green, oval leaves contrast well with other leaf shapes. Plant giant bacopa in groups, roughly 3-5cm (1.2-2in) apart.

The small, fleshy, pale green leaves of this bacopa contrast well with other plants in the aquarium.

▶ *Plant data*

Origin: Central America.
Maximum height: 20-40cm (8-16in).
Growth rate: Medium.
Area: Background, midground.
Light: Bright.
Temperature: 22-28°C (72-82°F).
Propagation: From cuttings.
Difficulty: 1, 2.

Difficulty Guide
1 Suitable for beginners.
2 Hardy and adaptable.
3 More challenging.
4 Difficult to care for and propagate.

BACOPA • BARCLAYA

Bacopa monnieri
Dwarf bacopa, Baby tears

This plant makes an ideal foreground plant for more open
areas, where it can be kept short and compact with good
lighting. The leaves are thick, oval and roughly 2cm (0.8in) long.
In low light conditions, the plant will grow taller with wider
spaces between the leaves,
which can look messy and
unattractive. Too much
pruning will also create an
untidy plant. Dwarf bacopa
is tolerant of water
conditions, hardness and
substrate, but will only
look its best under ideal
conditions.

*In low light some
stems will grow
rapidly, with larger
spaces (nodes)
between the
leaves.*

*Dwarf bacopa is seen to
best advantage when
several shoots are
planted in a group. To
propagate the plant take
a side shoot and plant it
in the substrate.*

*Bacopa monnieri
is suitable for
growing in hard
water conditions.*

Left: *Good lighting will allow
Bacopa monnieri to grow compactly,
with smaller spaces between the
leaves. This often produces a better-
looking plant and reduces the need
for regular pruning.*

Plant data

Origin: West Africa.
Maximum height: 50cm (20in).
Growth rate: Slow to medium.
Area: Midground, foreground.
Light: Bright, Very bright.
Temperature: 22-30°C (72-86°F).
Propagation: From cuttings and
side shoots.
Difficulty: 2.

Barclaya longifolia
Orchid lily

This attractive plant has long, wavy leaves with a reddish underside and olive-green topside, although the colours do vary across the leaf. The plant is demanding and requires soft water with plenty of nutrients, both in the substrate and in the water. High oxygen levels may cause it to deteriorate quickly. However, if it is properly cared for, it can become a very fine display specimen for the midground or background of smaller aquariums.

Above: The orchid lily should be given plenty of space in the aquarium. Its leaves and shape are quite distinctive and will contrast well with other plants.

▶ *Plant data*

Origin: East Africa.
Maximum height: 35cm (14in).
Growth rate: Slow to moderate.
Area: Background, midground.
Light: Bright.
Temperature: 22-26°C (72-79°F).
Propagation: By seed only.
Difficulty: 3, 4.

The large 'corm' is a storage area for nutrients and may produce more than one plant.

Difficulty Guide
1 Suitable for beginners.
2 Hardy and adaptable.
3 More challenging.
4 Difficult to care for and propagate.

105

BLYXA • BOLBITIS

Blyxa japonica
Japanese rush

Blyxa japonica is similar to *B. echinosperma,* but much shorter and harder to care for. In nature the leaves may grow fairly tall, but in aquarium conditions they rarely reach more than 5-8cm (2-3.2in). Even in the best conditions this plant may have a limited lifespan in the aquarium. For optimum care, provide very bright lighting and a soft water environment.

▶ *Plant data*

Origin: Asia.
Maximum height: 8cm (3.2in).
Growth rate: Slow to medium.
Area: Midground, foreground.
Light: Bright, very bright.
Temperature: 22-26°C (72-79°F).
Propagation: From side shoots.
Difficulty: 3, 4.

Difficulty Guide
1 Suitable for beginners.
2 Hardy and adaptable.
3 More challenging.
4 Difficult to care for and propagate.

Bolbitis heudelotii
African or Congo fern

This slow-growing fern produces large, stalked, dark-green leaves with a very solid structure. The plant will attach itself to solid objects, such as rocks and bogwood, and prefers to live in areas of flowing water. The plant is otherwise undemanding and can be kept in a wide range of water conditions.

Bolbitis heudelotii *is often sold already attached to bogwood. Place it in areas of water movement.*

▶ *Plant data*

Origin: Africa.
Maximum height: 35-50cm (14-20in).
Growth rate: Slow.
Area: Background, midground, or as a feature plant in the display.
Light: Bright.
Temperature: 22-28°C (72-82°F).
Propagation: By cuttings from the rhizome.
Difficulty: 2, 3.

107

CABOMBA

Cabomba aquatica
Yellow cabomba, Giant cabomba

This attractive plant produces many fine, feathery leaves. The yellow-green coloration is unusual and makes for an interesting ornamental plant. Due to the very fine nature of the leaves, it is vital that the water is clean and free from floating debris, and that algae is not allowed to form on the plant. Strong lighting is required to keep it looking healthy and compact. Stems should be planted in small groups in open areas, and at least 5-6cm (2-2.4in) apart, so that light can reach the lower leaves. The plant prefers water with a low pH (6-7).

 Plant data

Origin: Central America.
Maximum height:40cm (16in) .
Growth rate: Medium.
Area: Background.
Light: Very bright.
Temperature: 24-30°C (75-86°C).
Propagation: From cuttings.
Difficulty: 3.

Cabomba caroliniana
Green cabomba

This plant is the most commonly available *Cabomba* species, and the easiest to keep. The plant is highly adaptable to various aquarium conditions and does well in harder water and aquariums with moderate light. However, bright lighting will make the plant appear healthy and attractive.

▶ *Plant data*

Origin: Central and South America.
Maximum height: 50cm (20in).
Growth rate: Fast.
Area: Background.
Light: Bright.
Temperature: 22-28°C (72-82°F).
Propagation: Cuttings and side shoots.
Difficulty: 1.

Difficulty Guide
1 Suitable for beginners.
2 Hardy and adaptable.
3 More challenging.
4 Difficult to care for and propagate.

Keep the finely branched leaves free of debris, otherwise photosynthesis will be hindered. Good mechanical filtration, gentle water movement and small scavenging fish all help to remove debris.

CABOMBA • CARDAMINE

Cabomba piauhyensis
Red cabomba

The red cabomba is a demanding subject, but if given the correct conditions and care, the result is a stunning aquarium plant that creates a strong impact in any planted aquarium. As with other fine-leaved plants, clear, well-filtered water is essential. To keep this plant at its best, it must have a good, preferably iron-rich substrate, strong lighting, regular fertilisation, additional CO_2 and, ideally, a low pH of 6-7.

▶ *Plant data*

Origin: Central and South America.
Maximum height: 40cm (16in).
Growth rate: Medium.
Area: Background.
Light: Very bright.
Temperature: 24-28°C (75-82°F).
Propagation: From cuttings.
Difficulty: 3, 4.

Cardamine lyrata
Chinese ivy, Japanese cress

This unusual plant can be placed in the foreground, even though it reaches up to 35cm (14in) in height. It has a messy appearance and unusual leaf shape and often looks best when planted in small groups of three or four stems in between smaller, low-growing foreground plants. At higher temperatures and without adequate lighting, leaf growth may be stunted and stems will become weaker. Ideal conditions include a low temperature, bright lighting and a pH of 7-7.5. The plant is sensitive to many chemicals and does not do well in very soft water.

Difficulty Guide
1 Suitable for beginners.
2 Hardy and adaptable.
3 More challenging.
4 Difficult to care for and propagate.

This familiar aquarium plant is in fact a marsh plant that also thrives underwater.

Plant data

Origin: China, Japan, Korea.
Maximum height: 35cm (14in).
Growth rate: Medium to fast.
Area: Midground, foreground, or as a feature plant.
Light: Bright.
Temperature: 15-22°C (59-72°F).
Propagation: By cuttings, self-propagation.
Difficulty: 1, 2.

CERATOPHYLLUM • CERATOPTERIS • CLADOPHORA

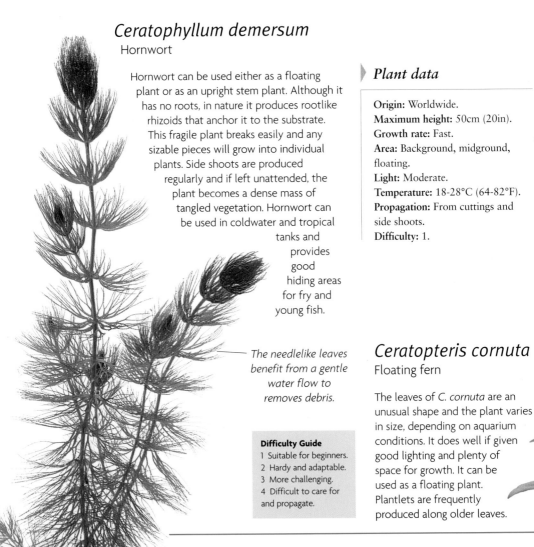

Ceratophyllum demersum
Hornwort

Hornwort can be used either as a floating plant or as an upright stem plant. Although it has no roots, in nature it produces rootlike rhizoids that anchor it to the substrate. This fragile plant breaks easily and any sizable pieces will grow into individual plants. Side shoots are produced regularly and if left unattended, the plant becomes a dense mass of tangled vegetation. Hornwort can be used in coldwater and tropical tanks and provides good hiding areas for fry and young fish.

The needlelike leaves benefit from a gentle water flow to removes debris.

Difficulty Guide
1 Suitable for beginners.
2 Hardy and adaptable.
3 More challenging.
4 Difficult to care for and propagate.

Plant data

Origin: Worldwide.
Maximum height: 50cm (20in).
Growth rate: Fast.
Area: Background, midground, floating.
Light: Moderate.
Temperature: 18-28°C (64-82°F).
Propagation: From cuttings and side shoots.
Difficulty: 1.

Ceratopteris cornuta
Floating fern

The leaves of *C. cornuta* are an unusual shape and the plant varies in size, depending on aquarium conditions. It does well if given good lighting and plenty of space for growth. It can be used as a floating plant. Plantlets are frequently produced along older leaves.

Plant data

Origin: Africa.
Maximum height: Up to 50cm (20in), usually 35-40cm (14-16in).
Growth rate: Medium.
Area: Background, floating.
Light: Bright.
Temperature: 18-30°C (64-86°F).
Propagation: By adventitious plantlets.
Difficulty: 1, 2.

Cladophora aegagropila
Moss balls

These slow-growing spherical balls of algae add a hugely original and interesting plant form to the foreground. Buoyed up by gases released during photosynthesis and respiration, they float to the surface, then sink again when the gases are released. They occur in shallow lakes, where the gentle movement of the waves forms the algae into spheres. Keep turning them regularly to maintain the ball shape.

The leaves of Ceratopteris cornuta vary in shape depending on environmental conditions and the original plant. The leaves may be finely branched or more 'whole' in appearance.

Plant data

Origin: Europe and Asia.
Maximum height: 3-10cm (1.2-4in).
Growth rate: Very slow.
Area: Foreground.
Light: All light conditions.
Temperature: 5-28°C (40-82°F).
Propagation: Division.
Difficulty: 1.

CRINUM

Crinum natans
African onion plant

This dominant, long-leaved plant can also be found in a narrow-leaved form, which makes a very attractive feature in any display. The wider-leaved form needs bright lighting and adequate nutrients, but the narrow-leaved one is less demanding. Both forms will reach up to 1m (39in) in length and trail along the water surface. Some herbivorous fish will not eat this plant. Provide medium-soft water and a good substrate.

In ideal conditions, the plant will grow rapidly and the long, highly indented leaves will trail on the water surface.

The leaves are quite tough and will cope with strong water flows in the aquarium.

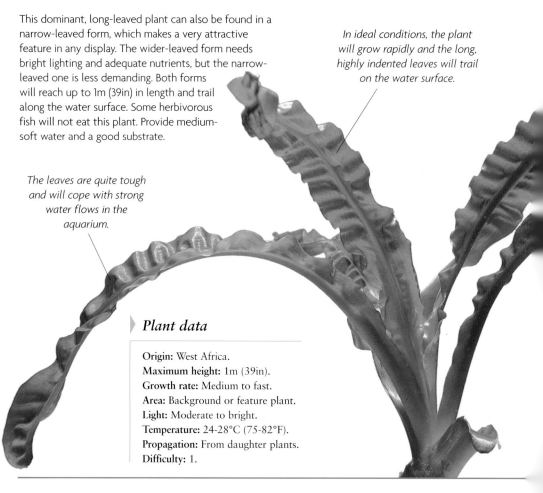

Plant data

Origin: West Africa.
Maximum height: 1m (39in).
Growth rate: Medium to fast.
Area: Background or feature plant.
Light: Moderate to bright.
Temperature: 24-28°C (75-82°F).
Propagation: From daughter plants.
Difficulty: 1.

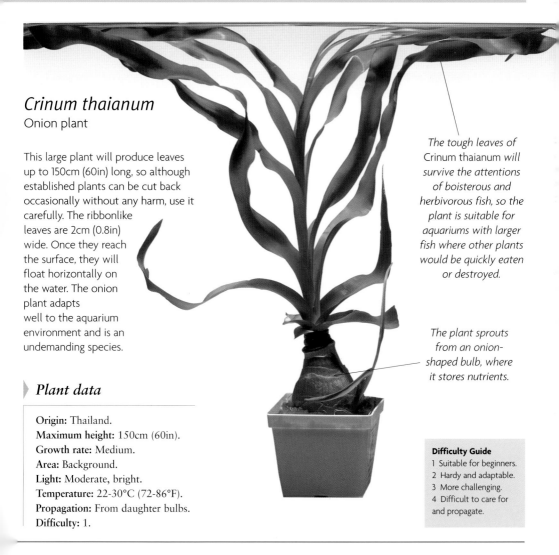

Crinum thaianum
Onion plant

This large plant will produce leaves up to 150cm (60in) long, so although established plants can be cut back occasionally without any harm, use it carefully. The ribbonlike leaves are 2cm (0.8in) wide. Once they reach the surface, they will float horizontally on the water. The onion plant adapts well to the aquarium environment and is an undemanding species.

The tough leaves of Crinum thaianum will survive the attentions of boisterous and herbivorous fish, so the plant is suitable for aquariums with larger fish where other plants would be quickly eaten or destroyed.

The plant sprouts from an onion-shaped bulb, where it stores nutrients.

▶ Plant data

Origin: Thailand.
Maximum height: 150cm (60in).
Growth rate: Medium.
Area: Background.
Light: Moderate, bright.
Temperature: 22-30°C (72-86°F).
Propagation: From daughter bulbs.
Difficulty: 1.

Difficulty Guide
1 Suitable for beginners.
2 Hardy and adaptable.
3 More challenging.
4 Difficult to care for and propagate.

CRYPTOCORYNE

CRYPTOCORYNES *are among the most popular and widely available aquarium plants. There are over 60 species and about half of these are relatively easy to keep in the aquarium. In nature, cryptocorynes are found in a wide range of habitats, including shallow, fast-flowing rivers, marsh areas, bogs and swampy conditions. The plants in this group are either amphibious bog plants or true aquatic plants, but all will adapt to fully submerged aquarium life. Cryptocorynes are not easy to acclimatise to an aquarium, but the plants are relatively hardy once settled, providing conditions are stable. Constant changes in temperature and lighting will make them susceptible to cryptocoryne rot, a disease in which numerous holes form in the leaves and the plant slowly deteriorates. A fine, heated substrate will improve plant health and encourage growth. Lighting requirements vary with each species, but many cryptocorynes are suited to aquariums with low light or subdued light conditions.*

Above: *Cryptocorynes are largely used for the foreground, where they will spread and cover a large area if regularly propagated. Here, they are also carefully positioned above each other to provide a striking display feature.*

Cryptocoryne albida

A few leaf varieties are available and the colour varies from light green to a reddish brown, occasionally with dark mottled leaves. The plant does not move well and will take time to acclimatise, but once settled, and if provided with suitable lighting and a nutrient-rich substrate, it should grow well. Very strong light can reduce leaf size.

Difficulty Guide
1 Suitable for beginners.
2 Hardy and adaptable.
3 More challenging.
4 Difficult to care for and propagate.

The very attractive elongated leaf shape looks best in large groups along the foreground.

▶ *Plant data*

Origin: Thailand.
Maximum height: 25-30cm (10-12in)
.Growth rate: Slow.
Area: Midground, foreground.
Light: Bright.
Temperature: 20-28°C (68-82°F).
Propagation: Runners, division.
Difficulty: 3, 4.

Cryptocoryne affinis

C. affinis from Malaysia is one of the most popular cryptocorynes and will adapt well to a stable environment. The crinkled leaves vary in colour and shade, usually sporting a light green glossy appearance. The plant will grow more quickly up to 25cm (10in) tall with increasing light, but may not appreciate very bright lighting.

CRYPTOCORYNE

Cryptocoryne balansae

This plant is similar to *C. affinis* but its leaves are much longer, elongated and highly indented. They may grow up to 40cm (16in), although 30cm (12in) is more usual. The plant does well in moderate lighting and hard water and is easier to care for once it becomes established.

Difficulty Guide
1 Suitable for beginners.
2 Hardy and adaptable.
3 More challenging.
4 Difficult to care for and propagate.

▶ *Plant data*

Origin: Thailand.
Maximum height: 35cm (14in).
Growth rate: Medium.
Area: Midground, foreground, or as a feature plant in the display.
Light: Undemanding, but does better in bright light.
Temperature: 25-28°C (77-82°F).
Propagation: From runners.
Difficulty: 2, 3.

Cryptocoryne beckettii
Beckett's cryptocoryne

The large leaves of this cryptocoryne are an interesting olive-green colour that contrasts well with other plants. Once established, the thick, bushy plant produced from adventitious plantlets often looks best on its own in the foreground or with other cryptocorynes. A nutrient-rich and heated substrate will improve growth.

Plant data

Origin: Sri Lanka.
Maximum height: 15cm (6in).
Growth rate: Medium.
Area: Midground, foreground.
Light: Moderate to bright.
Temperature: 25-28°C (77-82°F).
Propagation: Adventitious plantlets.
Difficulty: 1, 2.

The leaves and stems have a 'solid' appearance and provide hiding spots for small, bottom-dwelling fish.

Cryptocoryne cordata

The large leaves of giant cryptocoryne – up to 40cm (16in) long – vary in colour from light green to reddish brown and look effective when used in large, well-spaced groups. The plant requires a good substrate – preferably nutrient-rich and heated – to stay healthy. When moved, the plant is vulnerable and takes time to acclimatise. Once established in the right environment, it will grow well.

119

CRYPTOCORYNE

Cryptocoryne parva
Tiny cryptocoryne

This little plant will look very effective when used in groups along the foreground. With good growth, it is possible to achieve a lawn effect. However, the plant is not easy to care for unless you provide very good lighting, along with a reasonably good substrate. Well-established plants will spread relatively quickly through the production of daughter plants on runners. Can also be used as a bog or marsh plant.

When kept in large groups, the leaf shape of this plant will create a grasslike appearance.

▶ Plant data

Origin: Sri Lanka.
Maximum height: 5cm (2in).
Growth rate: Slow to medium.
Area: Foreground.
Light: Very bright.
Temperature: 25-28°C (77-82°F).
Propagation: From runners.
Difficulty: 3.

Cryptocoryne moehlmannii
Moehlmann's cryptocoryne

The green leaves of this easy-to-keep cryptocoryne from Sumatra vary in shape from oval to almost round and have a dimpled surface. If given plenty of room and good conditions, the plant produces a number of leaves, creating a compact plant that is ideal for the midground or foreground. Although adaptable, C. moehlmannii may not do well in very hard water. Provide soft-medium water, strong lighting and adequate CO_2 fertilisation.

Cryptocoryne pontederiifolia

This cryptocoryne has a bold leaf shape that gives it a dominant appearance in the aquarium. Once established, this undemanding plant is hardy and can grow quite large in good conditions. Moderate lighting is sufficient, although bright light combined with good fertilisation will increase its growth rate and overall size. The plant is similar in appearance to *C. moehlmannii*.

▶ Plant data

Origin: Sumatra, Borneo.
Maximum height: Normally about 20-25cm (8-10in), but can grow larger.
Growth rate: Moderate.
Area: Midground, foreground.
Light: Moderate.
Temperature: 20-28°C (68-82°F).
Propagation: Runners.
Difficulty: 1, 2.

Larger-leaved cryptocorynes can be used in the midground or around the edges of the aquarium.

Difficulty Guide
1 Suitable for beginners.
2 Hardy and adaptable.
3 More challenging.
4 Difficult to care for and propagate.

CRYPTOCORYNE

Cryptocoryne undulata
Undulate cryptocoryne

This attractive cryptocoryne
produces long, dark
green, highly ruffled
leaves, which make
it a good display plant.
As it ages it may produce
leaves capable of
reaching more than 35cm
(14in) in length. Low
light levels may
cause the plant to
produce light green
leaves. It does well
in hard water.

▶ *Plant data*

Origin: India.
Maximum height: 30cm (12in).
Growth rate: Slow to medium.
Area: Background, midground,
foreground, or feature plant.
Light: Bright.
Temperature: 22-28°C (72-82°F).
Propagation: By adventitious plantlets.
Difficulty: 2, 3.

Cryptocoryne siamensis

*Use this small reddish brown-leaved
cryptocoryne to contrast with green-
leaved plants in the aquarium foreground.
Additional substrate fertilisation will help
it to acclimatise and spread quickly. In
good conditions, C. siamensis will produce
numerous daughter plants through runners
and create a dense group.*

Cryptocoryne walkeri var. *lutea*

This popular cryptocoryne is commonly available and easy to care for. The plant often only looks its best once it has spread, creating a dense group of plants. Individual plants may look a little 'weak' on their own. A few leaf varieties are available, some of which produce brown veins and a reddish brown underside. The plant adapts to a wide range of conditions and should do well in any aquarium with stable conditions.

Leaves and/or stems that grow away from the main plant show that the plant is large enough to be divided.

▶ *Plant data*

Origin: Sri Lanka.
Maximum height: 12cm (4.7in).
Growth rate: Moderate.
Area: Midground, foreground.
Light: Undemanding.
Temperature: 22-30°C (72-86°F).
Propagation: From shoots.
Difficulty: 1.

Difficulty Guide
1 Suitable for beginners.
2 Hardy and adaptable.
3 More challenging.
4 Difficult to care for and propagate.

CRYPTOCORYNE • DIDIPLIS

Cryptocoryne wendtii

This tall cryptocoryne can be used as a background or midground plant and adapts easily to a wide range of conditions. The leaf colour depends on a number of factors, including lighting, and varies from an olive-green to slightly brown. The underside is usually a pale orange-brown. Plant it in spaced groups, allowing it to spread and create a dense clump.

Cryptocoryne
wendtii
'Brown'

Cryptocoryne
wendtii
'Mi Oya'

▶ Plant data

Origin: Sri Lanka.
Maximum height: 35cm (14in.
Growth rate: Medium to fast.
Area: Background, midground.
Light: Moderate to bright.
Temperature: 24-28°C (75-82°F).
Propagation: From shoots and runners.
Difficulty: 1, 2.

Cryptocoryne
wendtii 'Tropica'

Cryptocoryne willisii

This tiny cryptocoryne may reach no more than 4-5cm (1.6-2in) high in the aquarium and is often confused with similar species, such as *C. parva*. Its small size makes it ideal for the foreground area. If given adequate conditions, it will spread across an open area well. Adaptable and easy to care for if given adequate lighting and stable conditions.

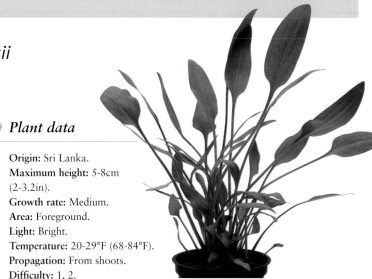

▶ *Plant data*

Origin: Sri Lanka.
Maximum height: 5-8cm (2-3.2in).
Growth rate: Medium.
Area: Foreground.
Light: Bright.
Temperature: 20-29°F (68-84°F).
Propagation: From shoots.
Difficulty: 1, 2.

Didiplis diandra
Water hedge

If planted in groups, this attractive a interesting aquatic plant will take o 'hedgelike' appearance. Good lightir an available source of iron are esser it is to remain healthy. In very stron; lighting, the uppermost leaves will t red, giving the plant an attractive 'ru look. It prefers a fine substrate. Place any cuttings in sand or a small-grade, lime-free substrate. Once cuttings hav been taken, the plant produces side shoots that increase its bushy appearar The plant does not do well in hard wat

▶ *Plant data*

Origin: North America.
Maximum height: 25-35cm (10-14in).
Growth rate: Medium to fast.
Area: Midground, foreground.
Light: Very bright.
Temperature: 24-28°C (75-82°C).
Propagation: From cuttings and side shoots.
Difficulty: 3.

ECHINODORUS

THESE AMERICAN PLANTS belong to one of the most common groups of aquarium subjects. There are more than 45 species in the wild and many of these are available for aquariums. Although there are a few solely aquatic species, echinodorus are predominantly amphibious bog plants that produce an aquatic form if kept submerged for long periods. The larger species are ideal for the background of spacious aquariums, and if given enough space and an open top, will quickly produce leaves above the surface. If the plants become too tall, you can keep them in check by occasionally trimming the roots and removing the taller leaves. *Echinodorus* species will propagate readily by producing numerous daughter plants on runners. Leave them in place until each plantlet has four or five leaves, then separate and plant them individually. Provide a nutrient-rich substrate, regular iron fertilisation and bright lighting. Given these conditions, echinodorus is one of the easiest plant groups to care for in the aquarium.

Above: *Most echinodorus plants have bold, oval leaves that create a striking feature in the aquarium. Some are smooth-edged, while others have distinctive wavy margins. The main plant shown here is* Echinodorus major, *the ruffled Amazon Swordplant.*

E. angustifolius *has a medium speed of growth and is straightforward to care for.*

The eventual length of the leaves of E. angustifolius depends largely on the growing conditions. The plant can reach 30cm (12in) in height.

The plant increases by producing side shoots.. To keep it in control pinch off the shoots and, if you wish, plant them elsewhere in the aquarium.

Left: E. angustifolius *has long, thin leaves that may resemble vallisneria or sagittaria foliage when fully grown. Use it as a back- or midground plant around the aquarium edges. It is undemanding, although good lighting and iron will help growth. The plant does better in harder water.*

ECHINODORUS

Echinodorus amazonicus
Amazon swordplant

*The thin leaves of the Amazon
swordplant from Brazil grow up to
35cm (14in) long. Use
groups of plants in the
background or plant it singly
in the midground. It prefers a
fine, iron-rich substrate and
medium-soft water. Remove
older leaves to keep the plant
looking fresh.*

Below: Echinodorus barthii *(double-red
osiris) slowly grows to 20-25cm (8-10in).
In good light, it will exhibit an
attractive golden-red
coloration.*

Echinodorus bleheri
Broadleaved Amazon swordplant

The broadleaved Amazon swordplant is the most widely available Amazon sword, partly due to its durability and ease of care. When established, the plant can take up a fair amount of space, so only use it in groups in larger aquariums or in tanks containing just a few plant species. Provide a good source of iron, both in the substrate and through liquid fertilisers. Does well in hard water.

▶ *Plant data*

Origin: South America.
Maximum height: 50cm (20in).
Growth rate: Moderate.
Area: Background or feature plant.
Light: Bright.
Temperature: 24-28°C (75-82°C).
Propagation: By adventitious plantlets.
Difficulty: 1, 2.

In good conditions, this echinodorus will regularly produce adventitious plantlets.

Prune E. bleheri *if it threatens to cut out lights to plants beneath it.*

Difficulty Guide
1 Suitable for beginners.
2 Hardy and adaptable.
3 More challenging.
4 Difficult to care for and propagate.

ECHINODORUS

Echinodorus cordifolius
Radicans swordplant

The leaves of this attractive swordplant are almost circular in shape, making the plant a dominant presence in a well-planted aquarium. Some colour forms are available with attractive red-brown mottled leaves. To keep the plant short and tidy, remove large and older leaves and trim the roots occasionally. Provide plenty of iron-based fertilisers. An undemanding and relatively easy-to-keep species.

Echinodorus bolivianus
Bolivian swordplant

This small plant has few demands and will do well in medium light, making it a good foreground alternative to similar, small yet light-demanding foreground plants. The leaves are light green, 10-12cm (4-4.7in) long and up to 1cm (0.4in) wide. An individual plant will produce many leaves and runners, eventually creating a 'carpet' effect. An iron-rich substrate and additional CO_2 fertilisation will help to keep it in good condition.

Plant data

Origin: North America, Mexico.
Maximum height: 40cm (16in).
Growth rate: Medium.
Area: Background, midground, or feature plant.
Light: Undemanding, but does better in good lighting.
Temperature: 22-28°C (72-82°F).
Propagation: From adventitious shoots.
Difficulty: 1, 2.

The unusual leaf shape of this plant makes it a good addition to a larger aquarium.

Difficulty Guide
1 Suitable for beginners.
2 Hardy and adaptable.
3 More challenging.
4 Difficult to care for and propagate.

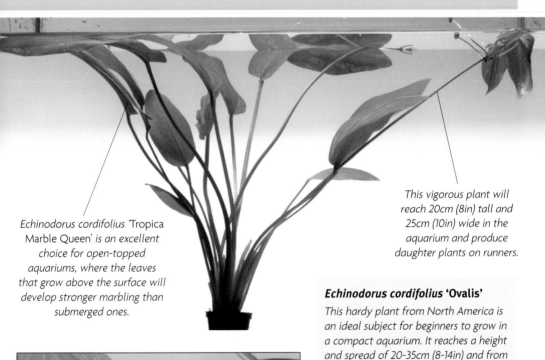

Echinodorus cordifolius 'Tropica Marble Queen' is an excellent choice for open-topped aquariums, where the leaves that grow above the surface will develop stronger marbling than submerged ones.

This vigorous plant will reach 20cm (8in) tall and 25cm (10in) wide in the aquarium and produce daughter plants on runners.

Echinodorus cordifolius 'Ovalis'

This hardy plant from North America is an ideal subject for beginners to grow in a compact aquarium. It reaches a height and spread of 20-35cm (8-14in) and from the rosette of oval leaves develops stems bearing adventitious plantlets that bend down towards the substrate. Provide plenty of nutrients for success.

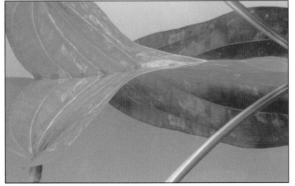

Left: Reflected in the water surface, these leaves of Echinodorus cordifolius 'Tropica Marble Queen' show the marbling pattern typical of this cultivated hybrid. Provide good lighting levels and CO_2 fertilisation to keep this plant growing well.

ECHINODORUS

Echinodorus macrophyllus
Large-leaved Amazon swordplant

This Amazon sword produces large leaves for its size, hence its common name. The leaves are typically up to 30cm (12in) long and 20cm (8in) wide, light green and robust in appearance. If given adequate conditions, it will produce a number of larger leaves above the water surface. Because of the substantial size of this Amazon sword, it works best as an individual specimen background plant in spacious aquariums. Ideal conditions for growth include a good iron- and fertiliser-rich substrate and plenty of light. However, the plant is adaptable and should survive well in most aquariums. Removing larger or older leaves and occasionally trimming the roots will prevent the plant from growing too large.

The large veins that transport gas and liquids can be clearly seen on many Echinodorus *species.*

▶ Plant data

Origin: Guyana, Brazil.
Maximum height: 50cm (20in).
Growth rate: Medium, fast.
Area: Background or feature plant.
Light: Moderate, bright, very Bright.
Temperature: 22-27°C (72-80°F).
Propagation: By adventitious plantlets.
Difficulty: 1, 2.

Echinodorus major
Ruffled Amazon swordplant

This large Amazon swordplant is similar in appearance to *E. amazonicus* and *E. bleheri*, although the leaves will grow much larger and are slightly ruffled around the edges. An ideal plant for use singly in larger aquariums. Provide a fine, iron-rich substrate and allow room for growth. Also known as *E. martii*.

These long leaves with fluted edges will add variety to any display. This plant will flourish in medium to hard water.

▶ Plant data

Origin: Brazil.
Maximum height: 50cm (20in).
Growth rate: Medium.
Area: Background or feature plant.
Light: Bright.
Temperature: 24-28°C (75-82°F).
Propagation: Adventitious plantlets.
Difficulty: 1, 2.

Echinodorus opacus
Opaque Amazon swordplant

The darker green leaves of this species make a welcome change from the more common light-green colour of most Amazon swordplants. It is adaptable and hardy, but can be slow growing when established and does not like to be moved. As with other Amazon swordplants, good fertilisation of the substrate and water, combined with good lighting, should ensure its continued health.

Difficulty Guide
1 Suitable for beginners.
2 Hardy and adaptable.
3 More challenging.
4 Difficult to care for and propagate.

133

ECHINODORUS

Echinodorus osiris
Red Amazon swordplant

The clearly visible veins and ruffled leaf edges make this swordplant more interesting than some others. The common name is a little misleading, as only the new, young leaves sport a slightly red-brown colour. *E. osiris* is relatively easy to care for and ideal as a feature plant in a larger aquarium. It does better in hard water than in soft. Provide plenty of iron, especially if the plant is kept in bright light.

Difficulty Guide
1 Suitable for beginners.
2 Hardy and adaptable.
3 More challenging.
4 Difficult to care for and propagate.

Although large, the leaves of this echinodorus are formed close together, creating a compact appearance.

▶ *Plant data*

Origin: Brazil.
Maximum height: 40-50cm (16-20in).
Growth rate: Medium.
Area: Background, Midground, or feature plant in the display.
Light: Bright.
Temperature: 22-28°C (72-82°F).
Propagation: By adventitious plantlets.
Difficulty: 2.

If this plant is allowed to grow out of water, provide adequate humidity to ensure that the leaf margins do not dry out.

Right: Echinodorus palaefolius var. latifolius *originates from the rivers and lakes of Brazil. It will thrive in standard aquarium conditions and reach 40cm (16in) or more in height and width. An excellent specimen plant.*

ECHINODORUS

Echinodorus parviflorus
Black Amazon swordplant

This adaptable and hardy Amazon swordplant is a popular, commonly available species. As the plant will only reach 25cm (10in) in height, it is an ideal alternative to many of the larger Amazon swordplants when used in a smaller aquarium. The substrate should be fine and iron-enriched. Remove older leaves if they become tatty and covered with algae.

The attractive textured leaves have distinctive pointed tips.

Used in the midground of the aquarium, the short leaf stalks of E. parviflorus will hide the stems of taller plants in the background.

▶ *Plant data*

Origin: South America.
Maximum height: 25cm (10in), sometimes taller.
Growth rate: Medium.
Area: Background, midground.
Light: Bright.
Temperature: 22-28°C (72-82°F).
Propagation: Adventitious plantlets.
Difficulty: 1.

Echinodorus quadricostatus var. xinguensis
Dwarf swordplant

This short, thin-leaved plant is ideal for use in the foreground. It will adapt to different levels of light and the leaf length will change according to light intensity. Given good conditions, the plant will grow and spread quickly, so initial planting should be well spaced. Yellowing of the leaves indicates a lack of iron.

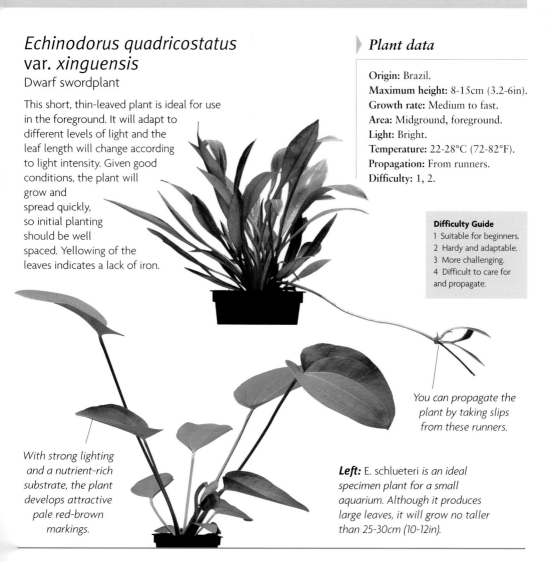

Plant data

Origin: Brazil.
Maximum height: 8-15cm (3.2-6in).
Growth rate: Medium to fast.
Area: Midground, foreground.
Light: Bright.
Temperature: 22-28°C (72-82°F).
Propagation: From runners.
Difficulty: 1, 2.

Difficulty Guide
1 Suitable for beginners.
2 Hardy and adaptable.
3 More challenging.
4 Difficult to care for and propagate.

You can propagate the plant by taking slips from these runners.

With strong lighting and a nutrient-rich substrate, the plant develops attractive pale red-brown markings.

Left: E. schlueteri is an ideal specimen plant for a small aquarium. Although it produces large leaves, it will grow no taller than 25-30cm (10-12in).

ECHINODORUS

Echinodorus tenellus
Pygmy chain swordplant

In good conditions, this tiny *Echinodorus* species will spread and create a lawnlike appearance across the foreground. Provide medium-bright lighting, a fine substrate and medium-soft water. When you buy them, many specimens exhibit the terrestrial leaf form, which is more oval shaped and on short stems. When placed underwater, the terrestrial form will lose all the existing leaves before growing aquatic ones.

Difficulty Guide
1 Suitable for beginners.
2 Hardy and adaptable.
3 More challenging.
4 Difficult to care for and propagate.

▶ *Plant data*

Origin: Northern and southern America.
Maximum height: 8cm (3.2in).
Growth rate: Variable.
Area: Foreground.
Light: Bright.
Temperature: 22-30°C (72-86°F).
Propagation: From runners.
Difficulty: 2, 3.

This is the aquatic leaf form of E. tenellus.

Echinodorus uruguayensis
Uruguay Amazon swordplant

A single plant may produce many leaves, creating an ideal specimen plant in most aquariums. The leaves are narrow (1-2cm/0.4-0.8in wide), start from the base of the plant and may have a slightly ruffled appearance. The plant normally reaches a size of 25-30cm (10-12in), but will grow even taller in good conditions. It can be kept in colder water, but may grow more slowly and produce shorter leaves, although it will still remain healthy. An undemanding plant suitable for larger aquariums.

Below: *Some cultivars, such as this E. 'Gabrielii', can be kept short by continually removing the larger leaves. This method is particularly useful in a small aquarium where a compact plant is required.*

The long, narrow leaves make an impact in the aquarium. Plant in well-spaced groups of three to five for the best effect.

▶ *Plant data*

Origin: Southern Brazil.
Maximum height: 30cm (12in) or more.
Growth rate: Moderate.
Area: Background, midground or feature plant.
Light: Bright.
Temperature: 18-28°C (64-82°F).
Propagation: Side shoots from rhizome.
Difficulty: 1, 2.

ECHINODORUS

Flowers are often produced on runners.
Where these flowers are formed, small
daughter plants develop, which can be
removed and replanted in the aquarium.

Right: Echinodorus 'Oriental' is a cultivated
hybrid. The plant is demanding and requires
very bright lighting and plenty of nutrients,
including iron. It will normally grow to about
20-30cm (8-12in), although it may be slow to
reach this size. The leaves often exhibit an
unusual, partially transparent, pinkish colour
that contrasts well with other plants.

ECHINODORUS

A daughter plant develops on a runner at the water surface.

In E. 'Red Flame' the oldest leaves take on a more shiny appearance.

Dark spots contrast with the lighter green leaves.

Left: Echinodorus 'Ozelot Green' is a fine specimen plant that will reach 40cm (16in) tall in the aquarium. It is easy to grow and tolerant of a wide range of water conditions.

Left: *With its red-dappled leaves and bold shape, Echinodorus 'Red Flame' lives up to its name in providing a colourful focal point in any planted display. Easy to grow, it will reach 40cm (16in) and more.*

Below: *The name 'Red Special' clearly explains the appeal of this cultivated swordplant variety. The copper-red foliage is markedly different to the usual green swordplant pattern and makes a great addition to any aquarium. The large, oval leaves often spread out, so give them plenty of room when planting. Bright lighting, iron-rich fertiliser and the addition of CO_2 all help to ensure that the plant looks its best and remains the 40cm (16in)-tall showpiece of your aquarium display.*

The leaves vary in colour, providing welcome variety in an aquarium display.

Below: *Lit from behind, the strong leaf ribs show clearly.*

ECHINODORUS

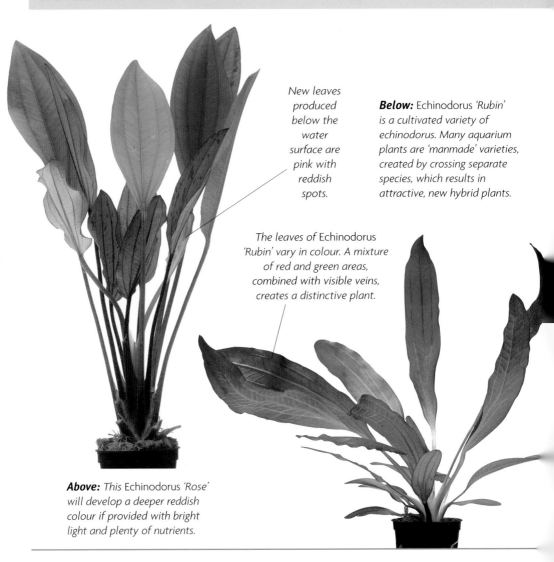

New leaves
produced
below the
water
surface are
pink with
reddish
spots.

Below: Echinodorus 'Rubin'
is a cultivated variety of
echinodorus. Many aquarium
plants are 'manmade' varieties,
created by crossing separate
species, which results in
attractive, new hybrid plants.

The leaves of Echinodorus
'Rubin' vary in colour. A mixture
of red and green areas,
combined with visible veins,
creates a distinctive plant.

Above: This Echinodorus 'Rose'
will develop a deeper reddish
colour if provided with bright
light and plenty of nutrients.

Left: The narrow-leaved form of E. 'Rubin' is equally stunning, with the same unusual reddish coloration. These plants are relatively easy to care for, although they require very bright lighting and may grow to more than 50cm (20in).

Above: The red edging of this leaf is unusual and creates a good contrasting effect when viewed against other leaves and plants.

Right: E. 'Tricolor' is another cultivated variety, with bold, oval leaves. In common with most large Echinodorus species, it needs good lighting and an iron-rich substrate for strong growth.

The leaves are attractive shades of green.

145

EGERIA • EICHHORNIA

Egeria densa
Elodea, Pondweed

This is one of the best-known and popular aquatic plants. Elodea is highly adaptable, fast growing and one of the easiest aquatic plants to keep. Ideally, it prefers harder water, but will adapt to a wide range of water conditions and temperatures. With good lighting, elodea can be kept in aquariums with higher temperatures.

In the wild, elodea will flourish equally well as a floating plant but will look better in the aquarium if planted in the substrate.

Difficulty Guide
1 Suitable for beginners.
2 Hardy and adaptable.
3 More challenging.
4 Difficult to care for and propagate.

Special note:

Egeria is found in many temperate and subtropical regions throughout the world as an introduced, or 'alien', species, meaning a species that does not originate from the area it is found in. In many places, particularly in Europe, fast-growing, adaptable plants such as Egeria can spread quickly and cause major damage to native plants and wildlife. Therefore, it is vital that aquarists behave responsibly and do not allow aquarium plants to reach open waterways, rivers and lakes.

Plant data

Origin: USA, now worldwide.
Maximum height: 50cm (20in) or more.
Growth rate: Fast.
Area: Background, midground.
Light: Moderate.
Temperature: 18-26°C (64-79°F).
Propagation: From cuttings.
Difficulty: 1.

Eichhornia crassipes
Water hyacinth

This potentially large floating plant can be kept in an open-top aquarium with reasonably bright lighting. The leaves are thick and waxy in appearance and may reach up to 15cm (6in) in length. The plant will spread rapidly and needs regular thinning. Water hyacinth is usually sold as a pond plant and does well in colder climates during the summer, but will die off during winter.

Left: *An overhead view shows the amount of cover provided by the plant, which is very welcome to the fish beneath the surface.*

Plantlets are often produced from shoots and in good conditions, these may need regular thinning.

Eichhornia azurea
Blue water hyacinth

The leaf shape of this plant from tropical and subtropical America makes a good contrast with many other aquatic plants. The leaves are long (10-15cm/4-6in) and narrow (0.7cm/0.3in). To minimise the need for frequent cutting back, keep it in a fairly deep aquarium so that it does not reach the water surface. It also requires a strong source of light and low water hardness to keep it in perfect health. Plant it in small groups of three or more, allowing plenty of room between the stems. Untrimmed, it will reach 45-60cm (18-24in) tall.

Plant data

Origin: Throughout tropical regions.
Maximum spread: 30cm (12in).
Growth rate: Fast.
Area: Floating.
Light: Bright, very bright.
Temperature: 20-26°C (68-79°F).
Propagation: From shoots.
Difficulty: 1, 2.

ELEOCHARIS • ELODEA • EUSTERALIS

Eleocharis acicularis
Hairgrass

This commonly available grasslike plant will vary in height depending on light conditions; brighter lighting will produce a shorter plant. Although easy to care for, good fertilisation and a clear, debris-free environment will prevent the plant dying back. Dense plants can be separated and replanted to encourage new growth.

The fine grasslike leaves collect undesirable floating waste from the aquarium water.

Above: *Hairgrass looks good planted in a sandy medium, with pebbles to add interest. Scavenging fish, such as corydoras catfish or kuhli loaches, will disturb the plant leaves and remove any debris that may collect there.*

▶ *Plant data*

Origin: Worldwide.
Maximum height: 25cm (10in), but usually 15-20cm (6-8in).
Growth rate: Medium.
Area: Midground, foreground.
Light: Bright.
Temperature: 18-28°C (64-82°F).
Propagation: From runners.
Difficulty: 2.

Difficulty Guide
1 Suitable for beginners.
2 Hardy and adaptable.
3 More challenging.
4 Difficult to care for and propagate.

Elodea canadensis
Canadian pondweed

Elodea canadensis is very similar in appearance to *Egeria densa*, and often sold as such, but does not tolerate warmer water as well as *E. densa*. Use it in groups of five or more for the best display. In good conditions, the plant will grow rapidly and may need regular pruning. Cutting will also result in the production of side shoots, creating a denser, bushier display. The plant is a good coldwater and pond subject; in tropical aquariums it may become weak over time. An adaptable specimen with no special requirements.

▶ *Plant data*

Origin: North America.
Maximum height: 50cm (20in) or more.
Growth rate: Medium to fast.
Area: Background.
Light: Moderate to bright.
Temperature: 10-20°C (50-68°F).
Propagation: From cuttings.
Difficulty: 1, 2.

Eusteralis stellata
Star rotala

Used in well-spaced groups and given good conditions, this plant can become part of a stunning midground display. Unfortunately, it is not too easy to care for. A soft-water, nutrient-rich environment, combined with strong lighting and a good supply of CO_2, will help to keep it in good condition. Taking cuttings will result in side shoots and a bushier plant. Even with the best care, growth may slow down or even stop.

▶ *Plant data*

Origin: Australia, Asia.
Maximum height: 30-40cm (12-16in).
Growth rate: Varies depending on conditions.
Area: Background, midground, Foreground.
Light: Bright to very bright.
Temperature: 22-28°C (72-82°F).
Propagation: From cuttings.
Difficulty: 3, 4.

FONTINALIS • GLOSSOSTIGMA • GYMNOCORONIS

Fontinalis antipyretica
Willow moss

This unusual little plant has numerous dark green leaves roughly 0.5cm (0.2in) in length, and spreads over rocks and wood in the aquarium. It does not produce normal roots but attaches itself to any permanent object. Willow moss prefers

moving water and does not appreciate hard water conditions. Ideally, keep it at a lower temperature; it is suitable for an unheated aquarium. Over time, the plant has a tendency to die off, even when kept in the best conditions. In this instance, you should replace it or separate the newer shoots from the main plant.

▶ *Plant data*

Origin: North America, Europe, Asia, North Africa.
Maximum spread: Continuous.
Growth rate: Medium.
Area: Midground, Foreground, or as part of a feature.
Light: Bright to strong.
Temperature: 15-22°C (59-72°F).
Propagation: From shoots.
Difficulty: 1, 2.

Glossostigma elatinoides

This tiny foreground plant usually reaches a height of only 1.5cm (0.6in) and once established, will spread to form a dense 'carpet' across the substrate. Its only major requirement is strong lighting; as long as other conditions are adequate, the plant should do well once established. Avoid placing it in shaded or covered areas. It can be used as a bog/marsh plant in damp situations. If conditions in the aquarium are relatively good, this is an excellent foreground plant.

▶ *Plant data*

Origin: Australia, New Zealand.
Maximum height: 1-2cm (0.4-0.8in).
Growth rate: Medium.
Area: Foreground.
Light: Bright to very bright.
Temperature: 22-28°C (72-82°F).
Propagation: From shoots.
Difficulty: 2, 3.

Gymnocoronis spilanthoides
Spadeleaf plant

This plant is often confused with *Hygrophila corymbosa*,
although the leaves are fleshier and less rigid than those
of *H. corymbosa*. The leaves of the spadeleaf can be up to
12-14cm (4.7-5.5in) long, so allow adequate space between
the stems when planting. New shoots
will rapidly grow to the surface, where
they may produce leaves above water.
Airborne leaves are thinner, more robust
and jagged along the edges. The plant is
relatively adaptable and easy to care for.
It can be kept in an unheated aquarium.

Difficulty Guide
1 Suitable for beginners.
2 Hardy and adaptable.
3 More challenging.
4 Difficult to care for
and propagate.

▶ *Plant data*

Origin: South America.
Maximum height: 50-60cm (20-24in).
Growth rate: Medium to very fast.
Area: Background, midground.
Light: Bright.
Temperature: 18-26°C (64-79°F).
Propagation: From cuttings, side shoots.
Difficulty: 1, 2.

HEMIANTHUS • HETERANTHERA

Hemianthus callitrichoides
Dwarf helzine

Apart from good lighting and nutrients, this plant has few requirements and will adapt to most water conditions. Before going on sale, many specimens are grown as floating plants to create a short dense mat of leaves. Providing the plant is regularly pruned, this appearance can be maintained. Without nutrients and strong light, the plant will quickly die.

Plant data

Origin: Central America.
Maximum height: 3-15cm (1.2-6in).
Growth rate: Medium.
Area: Foreground.
Light: Bright.
Temperature: 20-28°C (68-82°F).
Propagation: From runners and cuttings.
Difficulty: 2, 3.

Hemianthus micranthemoides
Pearlweed

Pearlweed has a delicate appearance, with small (1cm/0.4in), light-green, oval leaves, and is an ideal plant for the midground area of the aquarium. It adapts to varying temperatures and water hardness, but may be sensitive to some chemical treatments. Cuttings will often form side shoots, creating a dense appearance. Pearlweed is best planted in small groups.

Plant data

Origin: Cuba, Southeast United States.
Maximum height: 15-20cm (6-8in).
Growth rate: Moderate.
Area: Midground.
Light: Bright.
Temperature: 22-28°C (72-82°F).
Propagation: From cuttings and runners.
Difficulty: 2, 3.

Prune any extended stems to maintain a dense appearance.

Heteranthera zosterifolia
Stargrass

Stargrass is so called because of the starlike arrangement of leaves when viewed from above. This tall, bushy plant is ideal for background planting, or if regularly trimmed, the midground. The leaves are roughly 4-5cm (1.6-2in) long and 0.5cm (0.2in) wide. With good lighting, the plant is relatively easy to keep. Once the stems reach the surface the plant will produce numerous side shoots. If planted in bright, open areas, it will grow short and compact, creating a bushy effect.

Difficulty Guide
1 Suitable for beginners.
2 Hardy and adaptable.
3 More challenging.
4 Difficult to care for and propagate.

Stargrass can be trimmed to different sizes to provide variety in the aquarium display.

Plant data

Origin: Brazil.
Maximum height: 40-50cm (16-20in).
Growth rate: Medium.
Area: Background, midground.
Light: Bright to very bright.
Temperature: 24-28°C (75-82°F).
Propagation: From cuttings; self-propagation.
Difficulty: 2.

Right: *For the best effect, plant* Heteranthera zosterifolia *in groups, with taller specimens towards the back and shorter plants towards the front. Bright light will keep plant growth compact.*

HYDROCOTYLE

Hydrocotyle leucocephala
Brazilian pennywort

This plant is similar in appearance to *Cardamine lyrata* although the leaves are much larger, reaching 3-5cm (1.2-2in) in diameter. It adapts to most aquarium conditions, although it does appreciate good lighting. The shoots quickly reach the surface, where the leaves spread rapidly, cutting out light to the aquarium. To prevent other plants from losing light, be sure to prune Brazilian pennywort regularly. It will also grow in damp bog conditions.

Hydrocotyle sibthorpioides

This small *Hydrocotyle* species (up to 10cm/ 4in in height) requires very bright light and may be difficult to care for. In nature, it is normally found above water.

▶ *Plant data*

Origin: Southeast Asia.
Maximum height: 12cm (4.7in).
Growth rate: Medium to fast.
Area: Foreground, midground.
Light: Bright to very bright.
Temperature: 20-28°C (68-82°F).
Propagation: From cuttings and side shoots.
Difficulty: 1, 2.

▶ *Plant data*

Origin: Brazil.
Maximum height: 50-60cm (20-24in).
Growth rate: Fast.
Area: Midground, foreground, floating, or as a feature plant.
Light: Bright.
Temperature: 20-28°C (68-82°F).
Propagation: From cuttings; self-propagation.
Difficulty: 1.

The unusual 'branching' appearance of the leaves and stems makes this a distinctive plant in any aquarium.

Hydrocotyle verticillata
Whorled umbrella plant

Apart from good lighting, this plant has no specific requirements and should do well in most aquariums. It can be used as a foreground or midground plant and also as a bog plant. It is often sold for ponds during the summer months, but in most temperate climates it will die during the winter. Careful and continual pruning will eventually produce a densely packed spread of individual stems with variable leaf shapes. The leaves are light green and 3cm (1.2in) in diameter.

▶ *Plant data*

Origin: North and Central America.
Maximum height: 15-25cm (6-10in).
Growth rate: Medium to fast.
Area: Midground, foreground.
Light: Bright to very bright.
Temperature: 20-25°C (68-77°F).
Propagation: From side shoots.
Difficulty: 2.

It is clear that the arrangement of the leaves allows the plant to use as much available light as possible. Growing it in bright conditions will prevent the leaf stalks becoming elongated and the leaves too small.

Difficulty Guide
1 Suitable for beginners.
2 Hardy and adaptable.
3 More challenging.
4 Difficult to care for and propagate.

HYGROPHILA

SEVERAL VARIETIES of hygrophila are available for aquariums and some of the common species have different leaf forms. This group of plants is highly adaptable and will do well in most aquariums. Growth rates vary between species, but most are fast growing and will need regular pruning and/or thinning to keep them tidy. Cuttings can be replanted in the substrate and should quickly produce roots. Good lighting, plus CO_2 and iron fertilisation are important for good growth. In the wild, Hygrophila species grow in shallows above the water surface. If plants are allowed to grow above the surface in an aquarium, they may produce flowers.

Above: Hygrophila difformis (water wisteria) flourishing in a well-planted aquarium display. Bright lighting will help to keep the foliage looking good.

Hygrophila corymbosa
Giant hygrophila

Hygrophila corymbosa, a very popular, readily available and well-known aquarium plant, is highly adaptable and relatively fast growing. It is tolerant of a wide range of aquarium conditions, but may not do well in softer water. An ideal plant for any aquarium, it is not fussy about substrates or water quality. The plant can be grouped, but allow at least 5-6cm (2-2.4in) between shoots. It looks best when well spaced out and is ideal for the edges and corners of the aquarium. If the leaves begin to yellow, add more iron or CO_2. Can be kept in cooler water.

Plant data

Origin: India, Indonesia.
Maximum height: 50cm (20in).
Growth rate: Medium to fast.
Area: Background, midground.
Light: Moderate to bright.
Temperature: 20-28°C (68-82°F).
Propagation: From cuttings and side shoots.
Difficulty: 1.

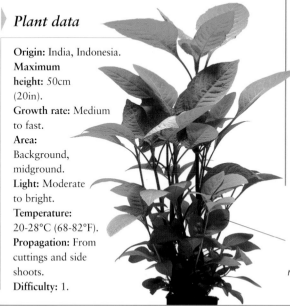

Above: *Hygrophila corymbosa 'Siamensis 53B' is an ideal beginner's plant. It is easy to grow in the aquarium, reaching 30cm (12in) or more, and is very hardy. In open tanks, it grows above the water, bearing blue-green foliage and blue flowers.*

Taking cuttings from taller stems will produce a more 'bushy' plant.

Difficulty Guide
1 Suitable for beginners.
2 Hardy and adaptable.
3 More challenging.
4 Difficult to care for and propagate.

HYGROPHILA

Hygrophila difformis
Water wisteria

This unusually shaped aquarium plant does well in bright light and looks best when kept in well-spaced groups of four or five stems. The leaf shape is dictated by aquarium temperature: at lower temperatures, the leaves are thicker and smaller; at higher temperatures, they are bigger and more divided. The leaves are large – up to 10cm (4in) long – so adequate space is a must. If the plants receive too little light, the lower leaves may drop off and the spacing between the leaves increases.

▶ Plant data

Origin: India, Thailand, Malaya.
Maximum height: 50cm (20in).
Growth rate: Medium.
Area: Background.
Light: Bright to strong.
Temperature: 24-28°C (75-82°F).
Propagation: From cuttings and side shoots.
Difficulty: 2.

Hygrophila guianensis
Guiana hygrophila

This shorter hygrophila is readily available but does not do as well in the aquarium as other hygrophilas. For best results, provide bright lighting, plenty of room and a nutrient-rich substrate. The light-green leaves are fairly large (10x2cm/4x0.8in) compared to the height of the plant, and have a delicate appearance.

▶ Plant data

Origin: South America.
Maximum height: 25cm (10in).
Growth rate: Medium.
Area: Background, midground.
Light: Bright to very bright.
Temperature: 22-28°C (72-82°F).
Propagation: From cuttings and shoots.
Difficulty: 2, 3.

Difficulty Guide
1 Suitable for beginners.
2 Hardy and adaptable.
3 More challenging.
4 Difficult to care for and propagate.

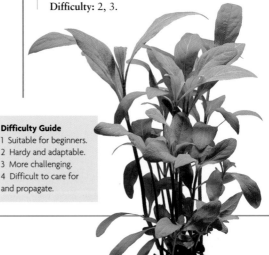

Hygrophila polysperma
Dwarf hygrophila

A commonly available and popular aquarium plant that is tolerant and adaptable. The leaves are shorter (4cm/1.6in) and narrower (1cm/0.4in) than *H. stricta* and *H. corymbosa,* and sport a light-green, sometimes reddish-brown colour. Regular pruning will keep the plant healthy. When it nears the surface, the leaves become red and compact. Ideal conditions include strong lighting and an iron-rich, fine substrate.

Hygrophila polysperma 'Rosenervig'

▶ Plant data

Origin: India.
Maximum height: 50cm (20in).
Growth rate: Medium to fast.
Area: Background.
Light: Bright.
Temperature: 20-30°C (68-86°F).
Propagation: From cuttings and side shoots.
Difficulty: 1.

The veins of H. polysperma varieties are often white in colour.

Hygrophila polysperma 'Big-leaf'

159

LAGAROSIPHON • LEMNA • LILAEOPSIS

Lagarosiphon major
African water weed

This aquarium plant, also known as *Elodea crispa*, is often sold as a pond plant and does well in cooler water. The unusual curved leaves give the plant a unique appearance, which may prove a disadvantage when you come to find a suitable place for it in the aquarium. Good lighting and cool water are its only major requirements; otherwise it is hardy and adapts to most conditions.

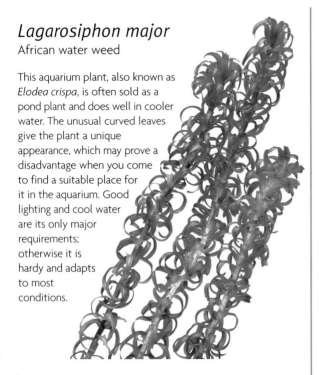

▶ Plant data

Origin: South Africa.
Maximum height: 50cm (20in).
Growth rate: Medium.
Area: Midground, foreground.
Light: Bright.
Temperature: 18-22°C (64-72°F).
Propagation: From cuttings.
Difficulty: 1.

Difficulty Guide
1 Suitable for beginners.
2 Hardy and adaptable.
3 More challenging.
4 Difficult to care for and propagate.

Lemna minor
Duckweed

Duckweed is adaptable, fast growing, hardy and has no specific requirements, but is often considered a pest. In good conditions it spreads rapidly, and a small group may develop to cover the surface of an average aquarium within a week. The light-green, oval leaves are 3mm (0.12in) long. If regularly thinned, the plant can be very effective in an open-topped aquarium. Duckweed often looks better as an ornamental plant when kept together with other floating species, such as water lettuce *(Pistia stratiotes)*, *Azolla* spp. or *Salvinia* spp.

▶ Plant data

Origin: Worldwide.
Growth rate: Fast.
Area: Floating.
Light: Undemanding.
Temperature: 10-30°C (50-86°F).
Propagation: By division.
Difficulty: 1.

Lemna trisulca

Lemna trisulca *is more attractive than* L. minor *and not quite as fast growing, although in good conditions it will still need regular thinning. The leaves – typically 1cm (0.4in) long and 0.5cm (0.2in) wide – are connected by short stalks and spread to create a dense mat across the water surface. Provide ventilation.*

Lilaeopsis mauritiana

Lilaeopsis mauritiana from the Indian Ocean island of Mauritius spreads across the foreground, complementing the broader-leaved plants behind and providing cover for smaller fish. Corydoras catfish provide a useful service by keeping it clear of debris. Strong lighting and a fine substrate will ensure healthy growth.

The plant grows 5-10cm (2-4in) tall, but regular trimming will keep it under control. Cutting it back to different heights will result in a more natural look.

Give this plant plenty of light and it will stay low growing.

▶ *Plant data*

Origin: Mauritius in the Indian Ocean.
Maximum height: 5-10cm (2-4in).
Growth rate: Slow.
Area: Foreground.
Light: Strong.
Temperature: 20-28°C (68-82°F).
Propagation: From side shoots.
Difficulty: 2.

LIMNOBIUM • LIMNOPHILA

Limnobium laevigatum
Amazon frogbit

The thick, waxy leaves of the frogbit are 2-3cm (0.8-1.2in) long and almost round in shape. This adaptable floating plant can be kept in open-topped aquariums or tanks with adequate ventilation. Given good conditions, it will spread rapidly and may need to be thinned occasionally.

Difficulty Guide
1 Suitable for beginners.
2 Hardy and adaptable.
3 More challenging.
4 Difficult to care for and propagate.

Plant data

Origin: South America.
Growth rate: Medium to fast.
Area: Floating.
Light: Bright.
Temperature: 22-24°C (72-75°F).
Propagation: From runners.
Difficulty: 1, 2.

Above: *Although the roots of this floating plant are not large and trailing compared to some floating species, they still provide welcome cover for surface-dwelling fish.*

Limnophila aquatica
Giant ambulia

Once established, this attractive, fine-leaved bushy plant is relatively easy to look after. Any difficulties you experience in keeping it can usually be attributed to changing conditions or the lack of a particular nutrient.

A readily available source of iron and fairly soft water (with a pH of 6-7) are particularly important. In good conditions and strong lighting, the plant will grow rapidly, producing noticeable growth almost daily. Stronger light will also ensure that the leaves are thicker and more compact. Do not take cuttings too often, as the original stem plant may begin to die back. Once cut back, the plant produces side shoots. Positioned in groups of individual stems placed slightly apart, giant ambulia makes an ideal background plant for the aquarium.

▶ *Plant data*

Origin: India, Sri Lanka.
Maximum height: 50cm (20in).
Growth rate: Fast.
Area: Background.
Light: Bright to very bright.
Temperature: 22-26°C (72-79°F).
Propagation: From cuttings and side shoots.
Difficulty: 2, 3.

Above: Limnophila aromatica *from Malaysia has narrow green leaves with purple undersides that intensify under bright lighting. It is easy to propagate by cuttings.*

LIMNOPHILA • LOBELIA

Limnophila sessiliflora
Dwarf ambulia

Dwarf ambulia is smaller, more robust in appearance and hardier than the giant ambulia. The leaves are arranged in whorls along the stem and individual stems should be planted in groups about 3-4cm (1.2-1.6in) apart to create a dense, bushy appearance. When the plant reaches the surface, it will grow horizontally across the water. It is adaptable to harder water and many aquarium conditions, making it an ideal plant for novices, although it does require a good source of iron.

Plant data

Origin: India, Indonesia, Sri Lanka.
Maximum height: 30-50cm (12-20in).
Growth rate: Moderate to fast.
Area: Background, midground.
Light: Bright to strong.
Temperature: 22-28°C (72-82°F).
Propagation: From cuttings, side shoots and runners.
Difficulty: 1.

Lobelia cardinalis
Scarlet lobelia, Cardinal flower

This plant is available in two distinctly different forms. The aquatic form featured here has short, thick stems with thick fleshy leaves that are often a deep scarlet-red on the undersides. Colour variations range from a light green on both leaf sides to a dark purple underside and dark green upper surface. The plant is hardy and undemanding and able to tolerate a wide range of aquarium conditions. Due to its slow-growing nature, it requires little care.
In its terrestrial form, the plant produces numerous purple-red flowers on stalks up to 90cm (36in) high. It is often sold as a marginal plant for ponds.

Plant data

Origin: North America.
Maximum height: Up to 30cm (12in).
Growth rate: Slow.
Area: Midground, foreground.
Light: Bright.
Temperature: 22-26°C (72-79°F).
Propagation: From cuttings and side shoots.
Difficulty: 1, 2.

Difficulty Guide
1 Suitable for beginners.
2 Hardy and adaptable.
3 More challenging.
4 Difficult to care for and propagate.

The thick, fleshy leaves are hardy enough to withstand the attentions of some herbivorous or boisterous fish.

LUDWIGIA

Left: Ludwigia arcuata *is a narrow-leaved form of ludwigia. An ideal bushy plant for the mid- or background.*

For this plant to produce red stems and red leaves it needs high light levels, but otherwise it is easy to grow.

Ludwigia brevipes

The small leaves of this plant can look very effective when used in a larger group towards the rear of the aquarium. L. brevipes is relatively hard to keep compared with other Ludwigia species, but strong lighting and a good substrate will help to maintain it in optimum health. The leaves are up to 3cm (1.2in) long and the uppermost or newer leaves may turn a yellow-pink colour.

Ludwigia glandulosa
Glandular ludwigia, Red star ludwigia

In the right conditions, this ludwigia will grow quickly, producing intensely olive-green/pink leaves that stand out well in a planted aquarium. Regular trimming will keep the plant compact and tidy. Given very bright lighting and good all-round conditions, it is easy to care for and will adapt to most aquariums. The leaves will grow to 5cm (2in) long. Best planted in groups of five or more. With good care, this plant can be very attractive.

The olive-green colour of the elongated leaves is a subtle shade that will contrast well with more boldly coloured plants.

Difficulty Guide
1 Suitable for beginners.
2 Hardy and adaptable.
3 More challenging.
4 Difficult to care for and propagate.

Plant data

Origin: Southern United States.
Maximum height: 20-30cm (8-12in).
Growth rate: Moderate to fast.
Area: Background.
Light: Very bright.
Temperature: 22-28°C (72-82°F).
Propagation: From cuttings and side shoots.
Difficulty: 2.

LUDWIGIA

Left: Ludwigia helminthorrhiza *is an attractive floating plant that does well in bright light. It can also be planted in the substrate, although it will grow quickly to the surface, with large spaces between leaf nodes.*

Ludwigia palustris

This undemanding ludwigia is a common aquarium plant that will adapt to most conditions if bright lighting is available. The reddish green leaves are formed close together, particularly near the surface, and vary in colour throughout the plant. Regular pruning will cause it to produce side shoots, making the plant appear more bushy. If cared for correctly, L. palustris makes a good display plant.

Although the structure of this floating plant appears to be based on individual plants on runners, it is in fact a horizontally growing stem.

Ludwigia repens
Creeping ludwigia, Narrow-leaf ludwigia

This plant, also known as *L. natans*, is found in a
variety of forms that differ in leaf shape and
colour. The most commonly available is a wide,
round-leaved form, that is light olive
green-brown on the leaf surface and
a reddish colour on the underside. The
plant is highly adaptable
and fast growing. As it reaches the surface, the leaves
become more compact and the stem grows
horizontally across the water, creating an attractive
overhead view. A number of rootlike shoots are
produced from the leaf nodes. Regular pruning will
keep the plant tidy and healthy.

*Given good lighting,
this plant is easy to
grow and an excellent
choice for beginners.*

Plant data

Origin: North and Central America.
Maximum height: 50cm (20in).
Growth rate: Fast.
Area: Background, midground.
Light: Bright.
Temperature: 20-28°C (68-82°F).
Propagation: From cuttings and
side shoots.
Difficulty: 1.

LYSIMACHIA • MARSILEA • MICRANTHEMUM

Lysimachia nummularia
Creeping Jenny

Creeping Jenny, an adaptable and commonly available species, is often sold as an aquarium plant as well as a marginal pond plant. In the wild it is found in ditches and marshy areas, where it is either partially submerged or growing in very damp ground. When kept in a tropical aquarium, growth may slow down and stop after a time. Replace the plant at this point. In the aquarium, good lighting is essential to keep the plant healthy. It tolerates a wide range of conditions and is ideal for the coldwater aquarium.

Plant data

Origin: Europe, Japan, North America.
Maximum height: 40cm (16in).
Growth rate: Medium.
Area: Midground, foreground.
Light: Bright to very bright.
Temperature: 15-22°C (59-72°F).
Propagation: From cuttings.
Difficulty: 1.

Marsilea hirsuta

This low-growing plant will spread via runners and shoots, creating an attractive foreground display. Although not always available, it is an attractive and adaptable plant and suited to a wide range of conditions. Provide a good substrate and bright light. Two similar varieties, *Marsilea drummondi* and *Marsilea crenata*, are also occasionally available.

Plant data

Origin: Australia.
Maximum height: 5cm (2in) or more.
Growth rate: Moderate.
Area: Foreground.
Light: Bright.
Temperature: 22-28°C (72-82°F).
Propagation: Runners.
Difficulty: 2.

Micranthemum umbrosum
Helzine

This compact, small-leaved plant will grow in a messy yet attractive fashion, and is best situated to the foreground of the aquarium in front of larger plants. Regular pruning will keep it tidy. The tiny (5mm/0.2in) round leaves are numerous and light green in colour. Although the plant needs very bright lighting when planted in the substrate, it can also be used as a floating plant and as a bog plant. Apart from good lighting, it has no special requirements.

Plant data

Origin: Central America.
Maximum height: 30cm (12in)
Growth rate: Medium.
Area: Foreground, floating
Light: Bright to very bright.
Temperature: 24-30°C (75-86°F).
Propagation: From cuttings.
Difficulty: 2.

Difficulty Guide
1 Suitable for beginners.
2 Hardy and adaptable.
3 More challenging.
4 Difficult to care for and propagate.

MICROSORIUM

Microsorium pteropus
Java fern

The popular Java fern is both versatile and easy to
keep. In nature, it exists both submerged and on the
banks of streams and rivers. Its roots are 'designed' to
attach to hard surfaces such as rocks and wood, and
this is how it should be grown in the aquarium. Java
fern adapts to most aquariums and requires little light.
It is a slow-growing
plant and older leaves
may become tatty
and blackened, at
which point they
should be removed. Java
fern contains chemicals
that deter most herbivorous
fish from eating the leaves.

Difficulty Guide
1 Suitable for beginners.
2 Hardy and adaptable.
3 More challenging.
4 Difficult to care for
and propagate.

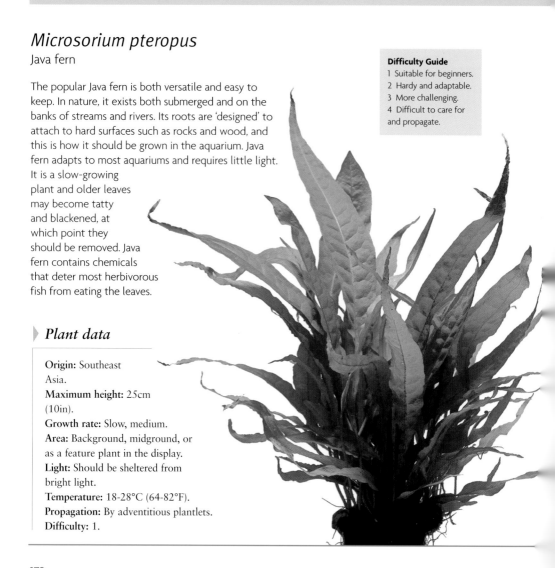

▶ *Plant data*

Origin: Southeast
Asia.
Maximum height: 25cm
(10in).
Growth rate: Slow, medium.
Area: Background, midground, or
as a feature plant in the display.
Light: Should be sheltered from
bright light.
Temperature: 18-28°C (64-82°F).
Propagation: By adventitious plantlets.
Difficulty: 1.

Java fern (Microsorium pteropus) is a popular aquarium plant for many reasons: it is hardy and adaptable and can be kept in aquariums where other plants would not thrive; the tough leaves and slow growth are suited to low light and low nutrient conditions.

Below: Microsorium pteropus 'Red' has the typical leaf form. Before planting, remove the pot and potting medium and tie the main root (rhizome) to a rock or piece of bogwood. You can place the plant in substrate, but the rhizome must be in open water.

Although left alone by most herbivorous fish, large destructive fish, such as oscars (Astronotus ocellatus), *or tinfoil barbs* (Barbus schwanenfeldi) *may still destroy leaves without eating them!*

Microsorium pteropus 'Red' will slowly grow to a height of 10-20cm (4-8in).

MICROSORIUM

With its distinctive leaf shape, this Java fern cultivar makes a fine specimen plant.

Black spots often form on the underside of the leaves. These are not damaged areas, but sporangia (spore cases), from which new daughter plants may develop.

Difficulty Guide
1 Suitable for beginners.
2 Hardy and adaptable.
3 More challenging.
4 Difficult to care for and propagate.

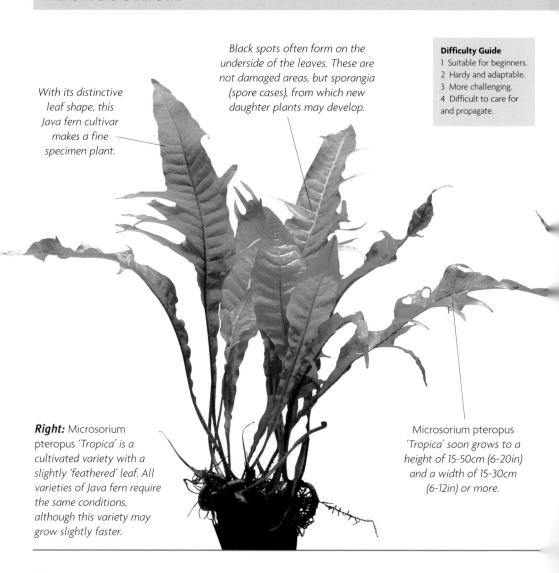

Right: Microsorium pteropus 'Tropica' is a cultivated variety with a slightly 'feathered' leaf. All varieties of Java fern require the same conditions, although this variety may grow slightly faster.

Microsorium pteropus 'Tropica' soon grows to a height of 15-50cm (6-20in) and a width of 15-30cm (6-12in) or more.

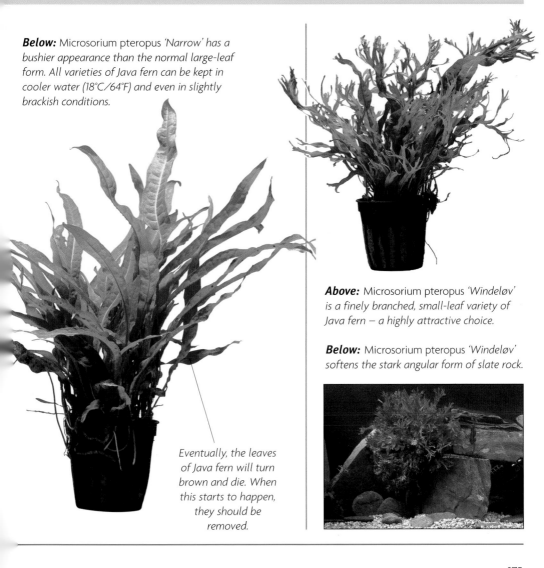

Below: Microsorium pteropus *'Narrow'* has a bushier appearance than the normal large-leaf form. All varieties of Java fern can be kept in cooler water (18°C/64°F) and even in slightly brackish conditions.

Above: Microsorium pteropus *'Windeløv'* is a finely branched, small-leaf variety of Java fern – a highly attractive choice.

Below: Microsorium pteropus *'Windeløv'* softens the stark angular form of slate rock.

Eventually, the leaves of Java fern will turn brown and die. When this starts to happen, they should be removed.

MONOSOLENIUM • MYRIOPHYLLUM

Monosolenium tenerum
Pellia

Originating from Asia, this stunning, small-leaved, fernlike plant is sold attached to rocks or purpose-made 'plant stones'. In good lighting and with reasonable CO_2 fertilisation, this 'living fossil' soon creates a pad of foliage in which fish love to rummage. Monosolenium does not have true leaves, but grows thalli, which look like webbed pads that fork as they grow. Small pieces break off, lodge elsewhere in the aquarium and start new plants. This unusual species can be tiered towards the back of the aquarium to create an impressive display.

Monosolenium is easy to grow, thriving in a wide range of temperature, water and lighting conditions.

Plant data

Origin: Asia.
Maximum height: 2-5cm (0.8-2in).
Growth rate: Medium.
Area: Foreground.
Light: Very low to very bright.
Temperature: 5-28°C (40-82°F).
Propagation: Division.
Difficulty: 1.

Difficulty Guide
1 Suitable for beginners.
2 Hardy and adaptable.
3 More challenging.
4 Difficult to care for and propagate.

Myriophyllum hippuroides

Like other Myriophyllum *species, this one must also be kept in debris-free water to prevent the finely branched leaves becoming clogged with algae. In very bright light, the leaves will turn a bronze-red-yellow. When grouping these plants, leave at least 5-10cm (2-4in) between the stems to allow room for growth and branching. Continual supply of nutrients is more important than rich fertilisation.*

Myriophyllum aquaticum

Brazilian milfoil, Milfoil

It is important to keep this common aquarium plant in water free of visible debris, which may clog the fine leaves. Providing you regularly add a multipurpose fertiliser to the tank, the plant should do well in most aquariums. It will produce side shoots, but over-cutting will damage it. In strong light, the plant may produce thick leaves above the surface. Milfoil does well in softer water and will grow without any adverse affects in acidic water conditions with a pH value as low as 5, although it will also do well in water with a pH of about 7.5.

▶ *Plant data*

Origin: South America.
Maximum height: 50cm (20in).
Growth rate: Medium to fast.
Area: Background, midground.
Light: Bright to strong.
Temperature: 22-30°C (72-86°F).
Propagation: From cuttings and side shoots.
Difficulty: 1.

Myriophyllum scabratum

The foxtail is an adaptable plant, well suited to coldwater aquariums. It must have clear water and good lighting if it is to thrive. It will produce numerous side shoots, which can be removed and replanted.

177

MYRIOPHYLLUM • NAJAS • NESAEA

Myriophyllum tuberculatum
Red myriophyllum

The stem and leaves of this plant vary between brown and red, depending on various aquarium conditions. The colour is highly unusual among common aquarium plants, making this plant a popular choice in planted displays. The fine, feathery leaves require clean, well-filtered water; any debris and/or algae will clog them and stop them photosynthesising. Strong lighting is essential for this plant. Do not plant individual stems too close together, otherwise light may not reach the lower leaves. The plant will spread across the surface and produce side shoots. Iron-rich fertilisers will improve growth. A very similar plant, *Myriophyllum mattogrossense*, is often available.

Plant data

Origin: Brazil, South America.
Maximum height: Up to 40cm (16in).
Growth rate: Medium to fast.
Area: Background, midground.
Light: Very bright.
Temperature: 22-28°C (72-82°F).
Propagation: Cutting.
Difficulty: 2, 3.

Najas indica

This delicate species produces numerous needlelike 3-4cm (1.2-1.6in) leaves in a spiral pattern along the stem. The leaves are brittle and easily damaged, so take care during transportation and planting. To keep the plants tidy, give them plenty of room to grow and provide fairly bright lighting. They can also be kept as floating plants.

Nesaea crassicaulis

This attractive plant is well suited to an aquarium with strong lighting and slightly soft water. It also needs additional substrate or liquid fertilisation and CO_2. A good source of iron will intensify the colour of the leaves. It is important that light is allowed to reach the lower leaves, otherwise they will quickly die and fall off. A demanding but worthwhile aquarium plant.

Given strong lighting, the upper leaves will turn an attractive golden-red.

Difficulty Guide
1 Suitable for beginners.
2 Hardy and adaptable.
3 More challenging.
4 Difficult to care for and propagate.

▶ *Plant data*

Origin: Africa.
Maximum height: 40-50cm (16-20in).
Growth rate: Moderate.
Area: Background.
Light: Very bright.
Temperature: 22-28°C (72-82°F).
Propagation: From cuttings and side shoots.
Difficulty: 2, 3.

NUPHAR • NYMPHAEA

ONLY A FEW tropical lilies are suited to, and available for, the aquarium. The most common groups include *Nuphar*, *Nymphaea* and *Nymphoides* species. Not all will produce floating leaves; some, including *Nuphar* sp., can be kept fully submerged without any damage to the plant. Tropical lilies need good lighting and those that do produce floating leaves must have open-topped or well-ventilated aquariums to keep the leaves healthy. If given a large open space and allowed to produce many floating leaves, they may produce flowers on the water surface. Many tropical lilies can be bought in bulb form without leaves. This is often a good alternative to transplanting fully grown specimens, which may suffer as a result of being moved. Bulbs may not produce leaves for several weeks and growth is slow initially, but will rapidly increase if given time.

Plant data

Origin: Japan.
Maximum height/spread: Leaves will grow 15cm (6in) long and stems normally reach the surface.
Growth rate: Medium.
Area: Background, midground, or as a feature plant in the display.
Light: Bright.
Temperature: 18-25°C (64-77°F).
Propagation: From side shoots on the rhizome.
Difficulty: 2.

Nuphar japonica
Spatterdock

Spatterdock's light green, triangular leaves contrast well with many plants in the aquarium. Ideally, it should be used singly in the midground with plenty of surrounding space. It has no special demands, but softer water will help to keep it healthy. Very bright light will prevent the leaves from reaching the water surface. To keep the plant short, simply remove the larger or older leaves.

Nymphaea lotus
Tiger lotus

This tropical lily makes an ideal display species in large aquariums and a fine centrepiece in small tanks. The leaves will grow up to 20cm (8in) long and, if left to spread, will quickly reach the surface, where they float and provide shade. The plant can be kept compact and submerged by continual pruning of larger and/or floating leaves and with bright lighting. The roots of established plants spread rapidly through the substrate and may be trimmed to keep the plant from spreading.

Plant data

Origin: East Africa, Southeast Asia.
Maximum height: To the surface.
Growth rate: Moderate to fast.
Area: Background, midground.
Light: Bright.
Temperature: 22-28°C (72-82°F).
Propagation: Daughter plants.
Difficulty: 2, 3.

Difficulty Guide
1 Suitable for beginners.
2 Hardy and adaptable.
3 More challenging.
4 Difficult to care for and propagate.

The leaves of Nymphaea lotus 'Zenkeri' vary in colour between specimens, although patches of purple or red-brown are common against green or green-red.

181

NYMPHAEA • NYMPHOIDES

Nymphaea lotus var. rubra
Red tiger lotus

This colour variety of the tiger lotus produces leaves that vary from a light green-red with reddish speckles to a darker green-brown with red speckles. It makes a good centrepiece and contrasts well with both tall, bushy or small-leaved background plants, as well as smaller foreground plants.

▶ Plant data

Origin: East Africa, Southeast Asia.
Maximum height: Will grow to the surface.
Growth rate: Moderate to fast.
Area: Background, midground.
Light: Bright to very bright.
Temperature: 22-28°C (72-82°F).
Propagation: From daughter plants on runners.
Difficulty: 2, 3.

Nymphaea stellata
Red and blue water lily

Although sometimes sold as red tiger lotus (*Nymphaea lotus* var. *rubra*) this tropical lily has smaller, spade-shaped leaves and will grow more compact, sometimes creating a better effect in a well-planted aquarium than red tiger lotus. The leaves will grow up to 12cm (4.7in) long and are a brownish pink to red in colour. If the light source is not bright, the plant will produce larger (20cm/8in) green floating leaves. As it ages, it may die back naturally, even under the best conditions. Apart from a good light source and moderate fertilisation, the plant has no special requirements.

Left: The leaves of Nymphaea stellata are more uniform in colour than those of N. lotus varieties, and their growth pattern may be more suited to an aquarium. Nevertheless, pruning some larger leaves may be necessary to keep the plant 'tidy'.

Difficulty Guide
1 Suitable for beginners.
2 Hardy and adaptable.
3 More challenging.
4 Difficult to care for and propagate.

Plant data

Origin: India.
Maximum height: 30-40cm (12-16in), sometimes to the surface.
Growth rate: Medium.
Area: Midground or feature plant.
Light: Very bright.
Temperature: 22-28°C (72-82°F).
Propagation: From daughter plants produced on shoots.
Difficulty: 2.

Nymphoides aquatica
Banana plant

This unusual little plant gets its name from the banana-shaped root sections that are used by the plant to store nutrients. These should be left above the substrate; the plant also produces 'normal' roots that will bury themselves. The heart-shaped leaves on short stalks are 10-12cm (4-4.7in) long. In shallow areas, the leaves will reach the surface and grow to 15cm (6in). The plant is relatively easy to care for but may have a limited lifespan in the aquarium.

Plant data

Origin: Southern United States.
Maximum height: 15-20cm (6-8in).
Growth rate: Slow to medium.
Area: Midground, foreground, floating.
Light: Bright to strong.
Temperature: 20-30°C (68-86°F).
Propagation: By adventitious plantlets.
Difficulty: 2, 3.

PISTIA • POTAMOGETON • RICCIA

Pistia stratiotes
Water lettuce

This common floating species is available both as an aquarium and a pond plant. In the aquarium, the leaves are 3-4cm (1.2-1.6in) long, but in an open environment they may reach up to 15cm (6in). The leaves are fleshy in appearance and have a covering of tiny hairs, giving them a velvety texture. Fine, trailing roots are produced below the surface and these provide good shade from lights and hiding places for smaller fishes. The aquarium should be either open-topped or have good ventilation, otherwise the leaves will become dried and damaged. An easy-to-care for species.

▸ *Plant data*

Origin: Tropical and subtropical areas.
Growth rate: Moderate to Fast.
Area: Floating.
Light: Bright.
Temperature: 22-25°C (72-77°F).
Propagation: From runners.
Difficulty: 1.

Left: *Small fish such as neon tetras will seek shelter in the trailing roots of water lettuce.*

Difficulty Guide
1 Suitable for beginners.
2 Hardy and adaptable.
3 More challenging.
4 Difficult to care for and propagate.

Potamogeton crispus

This unusual coldwater plant has a 'seaweed' appearance, which can look very effective in the right setting. The leaves will grow to 10cm (4in), have highly crinkled edges, and vary in colour from dark green to slightly reddish. If kept in temperatures above 20°C (68°F), the plant may become weak and die. Provide an iron-rich substrate and good lighting. This is also a suitable plant for a coldwater aquarium or pond.

Plant data

Origin: Worldwide temperate regions.
Maximum height:
Up to 70cm (27in).
Growth rate: Fast.
Area: Background, midground.
Light: Bright to very bright.
Temperature: 12-20°C (54-68°F).
Propagation: From cuttings and side shoots.
Difficulty: 2, 3.

Riccia fluitans
Crystalwort

This unusual floating plant spreads by progressive forking and produces a dense clump of separate plants that float on the aquarium surface. It is hardy and adaptable and can be kept in most aquarium conditions, including both unheated and warmer tropical aquariums. Once established, it can spread rapidly and will need occasional thinning.

There are many individual plants within a clump of crystalwort.

Plant data

Origin: Worldwide.
Growth rate: Medium.
Area: Floating.
Light: Bright.
Temperature: 15-30°C (59-86°F).
Propagation: By division.
Difficulty: 1.

ROTALA

Rotala macrandra
Giant red rotala

The deep red colour of this delicate, oval-leaved plant contrasts well with lighter green species, but bear in mind that the stunning leaf colour is dependent on strong lighting and iron-rich fertiliser. Transport and plant it carefully, as the stems are sensitive and easily damaged. *Rotala macrandra* is best planted in groups in front of taller species. Planting stems of various heights, with taller plants towards the back, will create a more pleasing group.

Plant data

Origin: India.
Maximum height: 50cm (20in).
Growth rate: Medium.
Area: Background, midground.
Light: Bright to very bright.
Temperature: 25-30°C (77-86°F).
Propagation: From cuttings.
Difficulty: 3, 4.

Left: The dense, colourful, 'paperlike' leaves of the giant red rotala are very attractive. Provide bright lighting.

Rotala rotundifolia
Dwarf rotala

This small-leaved species has an attractive, delicate appearance and is ideal for planting in groups in the back or midground of the aquarium. Lighting should be relatively strong. Given bright light and sufficient nutrients, the leaves may change from an olive-green to a pinkish colour towards the top of the plant. Cuttings should be at least 10cm (4in) long to ensure good growth. The plant is adaptable to moderate light and lower temperatures, although growth will be slowed. A few leaf shape varieties are available.

Difficulty Guide
1 Suitable for beginners.
2 Hardy and adaptable.
3 More challenging.
4 Difficult to care for and propagate.

Above: *Although the leaves are small and the distance between them is large, if planted in groups, this plant will appear quite dense.*

> ### *Plant data*

The leaves of this a sp. 'Green' will in light green, dless of lighting itions. However, bright is still important in · to maintain a fast- ing but compact plant.

Origin: Southeast Asia.
Maximum height: 50cm (20in).
Growth rate: Medium.
Area: Background, midground.
Light: Bright.
Temperature: 20-28°C (68-82°F).
Propagation: From cuttings.
Difficulty: 2.

187

SAGITTARIA

Sagittaria platyphylla
Giant sagittaria

Despite its common name, this plant is a low-growing foreground plant. The 'giant' refers to the leaf thickness (up to 1.5cm/0.6in) which is greater than in other similar species. This plant is easy to care for but requires bright lighting and a good supply of iron, either in the water or in the substrate. With time and space, the plant will produce a dense 'carpet' across the aquarium floor.

Above: *A healthy leaf such as this one should have a 'solid' colour and no transparent patches.*

Plant data

Origin: North America, Southeast Asia.
Maximum height: 15-20cm (6-8in).
Growth rate: Slow to medium.
Area: Midground, foreground.
Light: Bright.
Temperature: 18-26°C (64-79°F).
Propagation: From runners.
Difficulty: 2.

Sagittaria pusilla

This tough plant from Eastern North America is an ideal choice for the foreground, where a group of plants with overlapping leaves will look most attractive. The leaves vary in length from 5 to 15cm (2-6in), depending on water and light conditions. The plant is hardy, will tolerate hard water and survives in moderate to low lighting, although brighter lighting will keep it healthy and strong. Allow room for it to spread.

Difficulty Guide
1 Suitable for beginners.
2 Hardy and adaptable.
3 More challenging.
4 Difficult to care for and propagate.

Sagittaria subulata
Needle sagittaria, Floating arrowhead

There are several varieties of this very hardy plant that do well in most aquariums. They make ideal background plants. *S. subulata* can be used in harder water and even in slightly brackish conditions.

> ## Plant data
>
> **Origin:** Coastal areas of Eastern United States.
> **Maximum height:** 30cm (12in).
> **Growth rate:** Medium.
> **Area:** Background, midground.
> **Light:** Bright.
> **Temperature:** 22-28°C (72-82°F).
> **Propagation:** From runners.
> **Difficulty:** 1.

The leaves of Sagittaria subulata *are less tidy than those of other* Sagittaria *spp., but the plant's robustness makes it a suitable alternative for aquariums with less than ideal conditions.*

SALVINIA

Salvinia auriculata
Salvinia

The only special requirement of this plant is adequate ventilation above the water surface to avoid damage caused by the heat of strong lighting. The plant is adaptable and can be used in most aquariums to provide cover and shade for surface-dwelling fishes.

▶ *Plant data*

Origin: South and Central America.
Maximum height: 20cm (8in).
Growth rate: Medium to fast.
Area: Floating.
Light: Moderate to bright.
Temperature: 20-24°C (68-75°F).
Propagation: By division.
Difficulty: 1, 2.

Salvinia natans
Salvinia

S. natans is one of the most commonly available *Salvinia* species, and one of the largest. The leaves of this floating plant can reach up to 3cm (1.2in) in diameter, although they are normally smaller in the aquarium. Liquid fertilisation and good lighting are required for strong growth. Good ventilation between the light source and the water surface is also beneficial. This floating plant is a good choice for coldwater aquariums.

The leaves of Salvinia *species grow in pairs along short stems.*

Below: *The leaves of* Salvinia oblongifolia *are more extended and elongate than in other* Salvinia *species. This plant, found in the Amazon region, has similar requirements to those of* Salvinia auriculata.

The finely feathered roots of salvinia are designed to enable the plant to take up the maximum amount of nutrients from the water, but they also make good hiding places for fish.

Plant data

Origin: Europe, Asia, North Africa.
Growth rate: Moderate, fast.
Area: Floating.
Light: Bright.
Temperature: 14-28°C (57-82°F).
Propagation: Daughter plants.
Difficulty: 2.

191

SAMOLUS • SAURURUS • SHINNERSIA

Samolus valerandi
Water cabbage

In a stable environment, this delicate foreground plant, also known as *S. floribundus* and *S. parviflorus,* will do well once established. Provide plenty of light and well-fertilised substrate. The plant does best if given plenty of space.

▶ Plant data

Origin: America.
Maximum height: 12cm (4.7in).
Growth rate: Medium.
Area: Foreground.
Light: Bright.
Temperature: 20-24°C (68-75°F).
Propagation: By seed.
Difficulty: 2, 3.

Saururus cernuus
Lizard's tail

The attractively shaped and well-spaced leaves of this plant make it a good specimen for the midground of the aquarium. The leaves are oval to heart-shaped and a solid green colour. The plant has no special requirements, other than adequate fertilisation and good lighting.

▶ Plant data

Origin: North America.
Maximum height: To 20cm (8in).
Growth rate: Slow.
Area: Midground, foreground.
Light: Bright.
Temperature: 10-26°C (50-79°F).
Propagation: From cuttings.
Difficulty: 2.

Difficulty Guide
1 Suitable for beginners.
2 Hardy and adaptable.
3 More challenging.
4 Difficult to care for and propagate.

Shinnersia rivularis
Mexican oak leaf

The unusual leaf shape – similar to an oak leaf – makes this plant an interesting addition to the aquarium. The leaves are up to 5cm (2in) long and a dark green colour. In the aquarium the plant may grow rapidly and need regular thinning. Bright lighting will prevent the node distance between the leaves from becoming too large and keeps the plant compact. It will reach the surface and continue to grow under the water. Can be used out of water in a bog aquarium.

▶ *Plant data*

Origin: Mexico.
Maximum height: Up to 60cm (24in).
Growth rate: Fast.
Area: Background, midground.
Light: Very bright.
Temperature: 20-25°C (68-77°F).
Propagation: From cuttings and side shoots.
Difficulty: 2.

Shinnersia rivularis is easy to propagate. Simply trim off side shoots or cuttings and plant them in the substrate.

193

SPATHIPHYLLUM • TRAPA

Spathiphyllum wallisii
Peace lily

This tough-looking plant has recently become more popular in the aquarium trade. Although it is not a true aquatic plant, it is mentioned here because it will survive submerged and remain healthy for many months, sometimes years. The plant is slow-growing but easy to care for and well recommended for larger aquariums or those with large, boisterous fish.

Spathiphyllum wallisii *can develop into an imposing aquarium feature.*

▸ Plant data

Origin: Colombia.
Maximum height: 20-50cm (8-20in).
Growth rate: Slow to moderate.
Area: Background, midground.
Light: The plant is undemanding and will grow even in low light and shaded conditions..
Temperature: 18-28°C (64-82°F).
Propagation: From daughter plants.
Difficulty: 1.

Right: *Flowers readily form on healthy specimens of S. wallisii. Due to the large white petiole, they appear much larger than flowers of other aquatic plants.*

Trapa natans
Water chestnut

Water chestnut is more often used as a pond plant, but under good conditions and suitable lighting it can be kept successfully in the aquarium. Its major requirement is bright light for at least 12 hours a day and suitable above-surface ventilation. The leaves are 5cm (2in), roughly triangular and arranged in groups from a central, hairlike hanging root. The plant does better in soft water.

Difficulty Guide
1 Suitable for beginners.
2 Hardy and adaptable.
3 More challenging.
4 Difficult to care for and propagate.

Left: *After flowering,* Trapa natans *produces spiny fruits (nuts). In a natural setting, these detach and sink to the substrate, where they develop into new plants.*

▶ *Plant data*

Origin: Temperate regions.
Growth rate: Medium.
Area: Floating.
Light: Bright to very bright.
Temperature: 18-26°C (64-79°F).
Propagation: From runners and nuts.
Difficulty: 1, 2 (3, 4 in aquariums) .

195

VALLISNERIA

Vallisneria americana
Dwarf vallisneria

In the midground or background of the smaller aquarium, this short vallisneria makes a good alternative to the larger *Vallisneria* species. The leaves are highly twisted and will reach between 15 and 20cm (6-8in) tall. It is undemanding and should grow well in most conditions if given sufficient lighting.

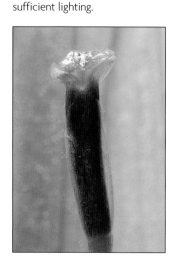

Above: *The tiny, white flowers of* Vallisneria *spp. are often produced in the aquarium, and may be formed on a straight or twisted stem that grows rapidly towards the aquarium surface.*

▶ Plant data

Origin: North America.
Maximum height: 20cm (8in).
Growth rate: Moderate to fast.
Area: Background, midground.
Light: Bright.
Temperature: 22-30°C (71-86°F).
Propagation: From daughter plants produced on runners.
Difficulty: 1, 2.

Vallisneria asiatica var. *biwaensis*
Corkscrew vallisneria

The attractive, tightly twisted leaves of this plant, also known as
V. spiralis and *V. tortifolia*, make a strong impact in the aquarium,
where it should be planted in close groups of 10 or more
individual plants. This vallisneria is ideally suited to the back and
sides of the aquarium and may require slightly more light than
other species. In low-light conditions, the spirals become more
widely spaced and the leaves may turn yellow. The plant is hardy
and adaptable, although it may not do well in very soft water.
A similar plant, *Vallisneria americana*, is often sold as corkscrew
vallisneria, but it has thicker leaves with fewer twists.

▶ *Plant data*

Origin: Japan.
Maximum height: 35cm (14in).
Growth rate: Medium.
Area: Background.
Light: Bright.
Temperature: 22-28°C (72-82°F).
Propagation: From runners.
Difficulty: 1, 2.

Difficulty Guide
1 Suitable for beginners.
2 Hardy and adaptable.
3 More challenging.
4 Difficult to care for
and propagate.

Below: *Twisted vallisneria
leaves add a stylish touch.*

VALLISNERIA

Vallisneria gigantea
Giant vallisneria

The fleshy leaves of this vallisneria may reach up to 1m (39in) in length and will trail across the water surface. The plant is relatively easy to look after and will adapt to most conditions. A good source of iron is important and this is best introduced through an iron-rich substrate. A lack of iron will cause the leaves to yellow. The plant may not do well in soft water at higher temperatures.

Do not allow the long leaves to cut out light to the plants below them. Prune as necessary.

Below: *Herbivorous fish normally avoid the strong leaves of this vallisneria.*

Plant data

Origin: New Guinea.
Maximum height: 1m (39in).
Growth rate: Medium.
Area: Background.
Light: Bright.
Temperature: 18-28°C (64-82°F).
Propagation: Daughter plants.
Difficulty: 1, 2.

Difficulty Guide
1 Suitable for beginners.
2 Hardy and adaptable.
3 More challenging.
4 Difficult to care for and propagate.

Vallisneria spiralis
Straight vallisneria

Straight vallis is one of the best known and most popular of the vallisneria family. The leaves may grow to 60cm (24in) in length and should be used as background planting or placed around the corners and edges of the aquarium. The plant will grow quickly and produce numerous daughter plants from runners. It can be kept in a wide range of aquarium conditions and in coldwater aquariums.

Vallisneria spiralis 'Tiger' (so named for the stripes on the leaves) has thinner leaves than the natural form. This is an easy plant to grow, adapting to a wide range of light and water conditions, and ideal for the smaller aquarium.

Plant data

Origin: Tropical and subtropical regions.
Maximum height: 60cm (24in).
Growth rate: Fast.
Area: Background.
Light: Moderate; grows faster in bright lighting.
Temperature: 15-29°C (59-84°F).
Propagation: Daughter plants.
Difficulty: 1.

VALLISNERIA • VESICULARIA

Vallisneria tortifolia
Twisted vallisneria, Dwarf vallisneria

This smaller vallisneria can be used in the midground or foreground of the aquarium and will spread rapidly, producing numerous daughter plants from runners. The leaves may reach up to 25cm (10in) in length, but usually only 15-20cm (6-8in) in the aquarium. This undemanding and adaptable plant is ideal for smaller aquariums. Plant it in groups of six or more individual plants, leaving space for them to grow.

Vallisneria is an ideal plant for beginners to try in the home aquarium.

▶ *Plant data*

Origin: Southeast Asia.
Maximum height: 25cm (10in).
Growth rate: Medium.
Area: Midground, foreground.
Light: Bright.
Temperature: 22-28°C (72-82°F).
Propagation: Daughter plants.
Difficulty: 1.

Difficulty Guide
1 Suitable for beginners.
2 Hardy and adaptable.
3 More challenging.
4 Difficult to care for and propagate.

Vesicularia dubyana
Java moss

Java moss is an adaptable and versatile aquarium plant. It can be used as a foreground plant amongst the bases of larger stem plants, be attached to rocks or wood, or simply left to its own devices. The moss will attach to any hard surface and spread in all directions. Regular trimming will to help to keep it in shape. It has no special requirements, although liquid fertilisation does increase the growth rate. Java moss can be used in coldwater aquariums and is ideal for breeding tanks.

Plant data

Origin: Asia, India.
Growth rate: Medium, fast.
Area: Foreground or as feature plant.
Light: Undemanding.
Temperature: 18-30°C (64-86°F).
Propagation: By shoot division.
Difficulty: 1.

Above: On close inspection, the tiny leaves of Java moss are clear to see. The plant attaches itself firmly to almost any object. In humid conditions, it can be grown above the water surface.

Below: This V. sp. 'Christmas' has branches that resemble fir trees.

GENERAL INDEX

Page numbers in **bold** indicate major entries; *italics* refer to captions, annotations and panels; plain type indicates other text entries.

PLANT INDEX

CREDITS

The publishers would like to thank the following photographers for providing images, credited here by page number and position: (B) Bottom, (T) Top, (C) Centre, (BL) Bottom left, etc.

Aqua Press (M-P. and C. Piednoir): 105(T), 106, 108, 180, 182, 182-3(TC), 183

Jan-Eric Larsson-Rubenowitz: 6-7, 88-89, 126, 156

Tropica (Ole Pedersen): 16, 39

William A. Tomey: 91, 92, 97

Computer graphics © Interpet Publishing:
Phil Holmes: 17, 53, 55, 76, 78, 80, 82, 84, 86

Stuart Watkinson: 9, 10, 11, 12, 13, 18, 20, 21, 22, 24, 38, 39, 40, 41, 43, 44, 47, 48, 52, 72, 77, 79, 81, 83, 85, 87

Index compiled by Amanda O'Neill.

The publishers would like to thank the following for their help: Martin Petersen of Tropica Aquarium Plants A/S, Hjortshøj, Denmark; Anglo Aquarium Plant Company, Enfield; Andy Green of Greenline Aquatic Plants of Spalding, Lincs; The Water Zoo, Peterborough; Kerry at Heaver Tropics, Ash, Kent.

Publisher's note